THE REAL
ENEMY IS
REALITY

A CHALLENGE FOR US ALL

by **Ted L. Cox**

Library of Congress Cataloging-in-Publication Data

Cox, Ted L., 1930-

Includes biographical references.

THE REAL
ENEMY IS
REALITY

A CHALLENGE FOR US ALL

by **Ted L. Cox**

To my partner: Diane Couture -

Once more to the woods, Diane,

For more moving adventures in….

The tangles and jumbles….

And riddles….

Of reality.

Preface

This essay is intended to be painful. It is not "another panacea." Painful reading is now necessary because too many panaceas and anti-demons and too much pain-avoidance have carried us to a dangerous place. We in Western Civilization somehow conceived the notion that we could look forward to an ever-increasing spiral of happiness in the future, for everyone. The remarkable increases in human comforts (not for everyone) that accompanied the industrial revolution supported this illusion. We began to value comfort more than each other; when the physical comforts didn't bring the expected pleasures, we became greedy; failed pleasure becomes greed. We felt cheated out of a promise: that the spiral of increasing happiness would continue regardless of our actions. We found instead (if we looked seriously), that we all have needs and wants that cannot be satisfied, by anyone or anything.

Our expectations were based on magical thinking. There is temporary comfort in magical thinking but like drinking, we pay a price when the "magic" wears off. Magical thinking makes us feel good temporarily but is delusional; it has inadequate foundations in reality. This essay is a challenge to increase our connections with reality so we may see the future more clearly and take more appropriate action. Therefore, it may be painful.

In a sense, I am picking up a flag from Francis Scott Key, my great, great, great grandfather, who saw great peril in concentrating power in the hands of a few who would rule the country for their own benefit. On this 200th anniversary of his "Star Spangled Banner," my purpose is to help our nation understand some of the unconscious motivation behind such ultimately self-defeating and earth-destroying behavior.

A large part of this unconscious motivation stems from the concept that reality is the real enemy and demon. It shouts at us that we are not *significant*. This terrifies us. We replace our terror with anger and create anti-demons or strategies to transfer our terror on to others; to transfer the suffering on to others. The effort is largely futile but it at least gives us the feeling we are taking action and not just suffering passively. But suffering passively equals despair, and despair has the potential for taking us to a new and better place where we can see the future more clearly. Our fear of insignificance is behind all of our problems. Our despair is like a shattering of the self that allows for reassembly in an improved format.

My hope is that if we can see the future more clearly, we can avoid some of the disasters and tragedies that await us otherwise. Many scholars more learned than I have warned us about the problematics of our cultures, but have not had a significant impact. Were I a pessimist I would not write this essay. I still have hope that love will prevail over madness and "Li'l Hitlers."

War occupies a large part of this essay because it is such an obvious manifestation of our lack of ability to perceive reality and act in reasonable ways. We seem to be addicted to warfare. But this is just the most obvious sign of our failing. In 1973, Ernest Becker pointed out how our unconscious fear of death leads us to violence that can only be explained as our attempt to deny our own animal nature, fallibility and death. That was 41 years ago and while there are — thanks to the Ernest Becker Foundation — many studies confirming this theory, it has yet to make an impact on social policy. Adam Phillips, a more contemporary social theorist, is quoted frequently in what follows and has also helped to explain some of our worst behavior. But again, no impact on policy to date that I know of.

Why? Because it is too painful. Certainly there are vested interests that present obstacles to apprehending truth, but the biggest problem is simply that we all got sucked in to the magical idea that we deserve to be happy, all of the time. When this fails to happen, we experience fear but cover this over quickly with anger. Next, we go on "witch-hunts" to find a "cause" for the anger we feel and punish the evil-doers. Hollywood helped to spread this magical lie, and Madison Avenue and drug companies make millions of dollars from this false promise to keep us happy.

But why are we so gullible? I think we can do better and so have written this essay, this swan song (I'm 83), in the hope it may contribute something to our ability to alter the course of our history in a better direction. It is the least I can do and the most I can do. So take a deep breath, summon your courage, and find out if you are strong enough to meet the challenge; to live somewhat closer to the truth. I apologize for the pain. If I thought there was an easier way, I would follow it.

Let's start with a painless journey back 200 years when we were a fledgling nation and "The Star Spangled Banner" was born.

CHAPTER 1

The Birth of "The Star Spangled Banner"

"O! say can you see by the dawn's early light…" Two hundred years ago, Francis Scott Key penned those immortal words of "The Star Spangled Banner" on the dawning of September 14, 1814. We can also see by the light of history that there have been 3,023 wars; another thing we should examine.[1] Key happened to be with the British fleet during the War of 1812 as he searched for the American flag over the ramparts of Ft. McHenry in that early morning light. The British had attacked the fort during the night — "Rockets' red glare, Bombs bursting in air" — and, for Key, the outcome was unknown. Had we surrendered the fort, our flag would have been taken down and might have been replaced by the British flag. Finally, Key was able to see a flag — and it was ours!

Eleven days before this, the 35-year-old attorney from Washington had sailed out of Baltimore under a flag of truce to search for the British fleet; he knew it to be somewhere on Chesapeake Bay. He had been chosen by President Madison to negotiate with the British for the release of an American civilian whom we felt had been wrongly imprisoned by the British. He was accompanied by a Colonel Skinner, a U.S. Agent for Parole of Prisoners during the war. Days later they located the British fleet near the mouths of the Potomac and Patuxent Rivers, about 100 miles south of Baltimore. The prisoner, a Doctor Beanes, was being held by the British on one of their warships.

The negotiation started badly with British Admiral Cochrane saying he planned to hang the doctor from a yardarm of his ship. Like the good attorney he was, Key never revealed the details of these negotiations. So, as in all closed-door hearings, we don't know what other threats and promises were made during the deliberations. We do know that Key and Skinner carried letters from wounded British soldiers testifying to the good medical treatment they had received from American doctors. With this information and Key's diplomacy,[2] the British finally agreed to release Doctor Beanes.[3]

During these negotiations, Key and Skinner had sailed with the British toward Baltimore, and witnessed the preparations for the attack on the city. Therefore, the British insisted the three men remain tied up alongside British ships, guarded by British marines, so they could not warn Baltimore of the coming invasion.

Ft. McHenry survived the bombardment and refused to surrender; a British force attempting to take the fort from the rear at night was repulsed with substantial loss of British lives. Next, the invading troops marching on Baltimore from the mainland withdrew. Only then were Key, Colonel Skinner and Doctor Beanes permitted to return to Baltimore, and the British sailed away. This is how Francis Scott Key came to be with the ships of the enemy, watching the bombardment of Ft. McHenry and searching anxiously "by the dawn's early light" for the sight of a flag. This was the birth of "The Star Spangled Banner."

My own peculiar vantage point on American society stems from 83 years of living, studying and working in our country as a U.S. Navy surveyor, government clerk, diver, sociologist and finally, psychoanalyst. I never experienced a serious commitment at any of the various institutions where I worked, studied, or taught. I saw the various comforts and constraints available and chose, through arrogance as much as clarity, to remain suspicious and uncommitted. I never seemed to fit in anywhere. The "buzzwords" at each institution, or what Chris Hedges[4] calls "subcultural linguistic codes of identification," always seemed to me contrived and more like group attempts at proclaiming their superiority; bromides of one kind or another. My nickname in my college fraternity was "Lost." Later, I learned that almost all culture is an attempt to hide reality; to conceal the source of our terrors. I was so naïve, terrified and baffled by life that I felt truth was the over-riding consideration in all human affairs. It still is for me. However, this conviction has caused me some grief in different settings, such as the corporate sector where honesty is a liability. I was an unintentional "whistle-blower" there (to be described below). The various skullduggeries I encountered in academia deserve another publication.

Hence, like my grandfather, Frank Key on the British ships, I have the perspective of the outsider; or rather, of one that is beside the others but not committed to their "cause." It seemed to me quite early in life that loyalty to institutional hierarchies, norms and values (even when feigned) entails the sacrifice of some individuality and a certain bias that obscures truth: what Adam Phillips calls a "defensive knowingness" (Adam Phillips, *Terrors and Experts*, p. 87). Empty-headed patriotism as in, "My country right or wrong" is one example. Still, I recognize that we all need consolation, or a comfort zone; membership in a group, especially large powerful institutions, either secular or religious, provides a quota of consolation and meaning not otherwise available. Adam Phillips puts it this way: "Meaning requires accomplices" (Phillips, p. 12). We are social animals; this is our great strength when group action is required and our great weakness when truth is required.

Our turmoil and danger today is less specific than it was on that September morning in 1814, but it's just as perilous and it is worldwide. What are the chances that we will surrender our world to the greed of people and nations, and end in premature annihilation because of a struggle to capture secular and/or religious delusions of happiness, immortality and power? I will explore and elaborate on this question and present a monologue with my grandfather, Key, about what has happened in our country since his day. But first, some bicentennial thoughts on living in our world, and how could there have been 3,023 wars?

ENDNOTES

1   War is defined here as conflict in which at least 1000 people die.

2   Key, at 35, was a relatively unknown Washington attorney and amateur poet but subsequently became widely recognized for his skills in negotiation and diplomacy.

3   We do have Key's opinion of British officers in general expressed in a letter to his good friend, John Randolph, shortly after the liberation of Doctor Beanes: "... illiberal, ignorant and vulgar, and ... filled with a spirit of malignity against everything American." (Edward S. Delaplaine, *Francis Scott Key*. 1937, p. 173.)

4   Page 132 of "American Fascists."

CHAPTER 2

The Big Secret

The best-kept secret in Western culture is that life is intrinsically difficult — for all of us, for everyone. What our culture would have us believe is that when life is difficult, it's our fault. This paradigm of cognitive capture is the ruling elite's substitute for control though religion. The argument is that if you're not happy and your life is intrinsically difficult, it's because you don't have enough money, or power, or beauty, or sex[1], or fame, or faith — because you're not a celebrity. That's not true. It is intrinsically difficult because "we, like all animals, are a project that issues in nothing" (Leo Bersani and Adam Phillips, *Intimacies*, 2008, p. 114). And we counter this knowledge (however deeply buried in the unconscious it may be) by trying to be more important than others. Everyone wants to be important — and *no one is*. Or at least, no one ever feels important enough to conquer their fears of change: loss of significance and death. No one will remember your name. And yet, we are tantalized because we taste "importance" in our lives from time to time. We were important to our parents, even if they hated us.[2] If we can have a *little* importance, why not a *lot*? If we can have it *sometime*, why not *all* of the time? Why not all of it, all of the time?[3]

Society holds out many different ways to achieve, or at least to pursue, importance. But our importance in society is always ambiguous; we're never sure just how important we are. It constantly shifts and morphs into things we cannot totally understand or control; both our own evaluation and that of others, and the interaction between the two. This collision between our own powerful but vague feelings of importance and the shifting importance assigned to us by different segments of society takes many different forms.

This idea has been around for a long time, as in Herman Melville's "Moby Dick" (1851)[4]; Henry David Thoreau's "Walden" "most men lead lives of quiet desperation" (1854); and Simone Weil's "Gravity and Grace" (1952): "There is, as it were, a phagocytosis in the soul: everything which is threatened by time secrets falsehood in order not to die..." The difficulty of living is only recently gaining the recognition it deserves, as in "My Anxious, Twitchy, Phobic Life" by Scott Stossel (Jan./Feb. 2014 *The Atlantic*); and "It's hard not to be afraid. Be less afraid" from Susan Sontag. The good news is that this constant tension built into the human condition is responsible for many of the good things we create for society, and it helps turn the wheels of our economy. It makes life very interesting. We work very hard in order to confirm and improve our feelings of importance.

Most individual and social behavior is influenced by this phenomenon: life is difficult and we try to hide it; we lie about it. Quoting Adam Phillips: "… we are most resistant to talking about the things that matter most to us," and "… we are endangered by our optimism." (Phillips, *On Balance*, p. 77 and 80) "… the function of culture is to kill curiosity …" (*The Beast in the Nursery*, p. 22). Meanwhile, we have become so busy trying to be important that there is an epidemic of 'celebrityitis.' I define celebrityitis as the illusion of being a celebrity and the expectation of a constant celebration. The particular kind of competition reflected in societies where celebrityitis is dominant is one based on quantities of evidence for celebrity status. We count number of friends on Facebook; number of hits on a web site; number of dollars in the bank; number of performances (public or private) and readings on applause meters or that equivalent for evaluations. To the extent that we succeed with this, we are so busy that we avoid despair and miss out on love, which is the only real consolation for being human.

The "cultural tide" seems to be changing to a place where contributions to culture are not as important as just perfecting the technique of appearing to be a celebrity; conducting good performances.

It is also apparent that this epidemic of celebrityitis, this cognitive capture, provides a structure for our lives and our society, which is less restrictive than some from the past. It provides a diversion from difficulty, and even sometimes a shelter where we can find room to practice the "art of informality:" the exploration of new ideas about how to understand the past, the future and our relationships with each other. While these are still quite rare, examples can be found in organizations like Focusing.org; ErnestBecker.org; psychohistory.us and leftforum.org. This is similar to the structure of Christianity, which, though highly restrictive in some times and places (e.g., the Inquisition) still provided opportunities for the growth of wisdom over time.

To the extent that we do realize this difficulty, we have two basic responses: love life in spite of its difficulty or be angry about it. The anger may lead in two different directions: we may use it to hate life and other people because they are so difficult, or we may cultivate courage from the anger and then do what we can to make life better. These two mostly unconscious patterns are seldom found in pure form, but rather mixed together in various proportions in individuals and societies. This is a simple explanation for much of human behavior, including war, and — following the principle of Occam's Razor — should be fully explored before we turn to more complicated and especially magical explanations. Many centuries ago, St. Augustine observed that "Hope has two beautiful daughters: anger and courage. Anger about the way life is, and the courage to do something about it." For without the anger, motivation will be in short supply. And we need tremendous motivation in order to sustain hope and make the best we can out of this very difficult human situation.

• • •

Another important dimension of personality begins with the way in which we are first recognized as "beings." This often determines whether we pursue an identity mostly as an important victor or as important victim; whether the anger is focused outward or inward. Again, pure forms are rare; we mix and match. If we experience ourselves as weak but important when we are hurt, sick or dying, we tend to incorporate that into who we are and how we should channel our energies and expectations in the future in order to "be." If we feel we have power, like the power to make parents feel guilty because they are not living up to the social expectations of good parenting, then we tend to experience ourselves as victors. We are so desperate for importance, significance and relevance that we turn to whatever channel is available from our experience and our environment. The great fear for all is that we might sink down into the great anonymous sea of the unwashed masses and become invisible.

Historically, we seem to revel in magical feel-better

explanations supported by group consensus. And perhaps we cannot function without some element of this in culture: some magical refuge for periodic retreats to a world that makes sense and where we are significant — or at least where we can forget about the reality-struggle for a time. Self-righteous institutions (religious or secular), alcohol, drugs, loud music, busy social interaction, busy vacations ... all provide some refuge from reality. More informal and spontaneous social interaction can be risky as in Sartre's admonition that "Hell is other people." Another side of the "people coin" comes from Dostoyevsky via Chris Hedges (*Losing Moses on the Freeway*, p. 18) "[Hell is] the suffering of being no longer [or never] able to love."[5]

Many fear drowning in the sea of the unwashed masses if they venture into intimate and informal relationships with others. But if any of these magical reality-refuges or "escape mechanisms" come to dominate our lives and culture, or become a permanent refuge, the human experiment may fail because reality has not been given the respect it warrants. What is the optimum ratio of refuge-time versus time spent in the struggle with reality? We experiment now in a haphazard way to find answers. Most of us, I believe, can tolerate more reality than we think we can, especially given that the average American watches almost 3 hours of TV each day. "Our fear is always in excess of the object's capacity to satisfy it." (Adam Phillips, *Promises, Promises*, p. 51).

Scott Stossel writes in the January/February 2014 issue

of *The Atlantic* about "Surviving Anxiety" of his anxious, twitchy, phobic life. Sensitive, intelligent people have more trouble than others swallowing the social fantasies and beliefs (as embedded in culture) that disguise reality. At times culture can seem shallow at best, as in original sin and loving and/or punishing Gods, and despicable at worst, as in greed, abuse of power, violence, racism and sexism. Add to this our collision with reality after an infancy of believing our parents were omniscient and omnipotent and totally devoted to our well-being: more indigestible "food" we have to contend with. These anxious people can make significant contributions to culture, but pay a high price for their objectivity and lack of commitment and tenuous connections. In Stossel's case, the life-long struggle with fear of vomiting could be framed as a symbol of his inability to "digest" the conflicting fantasies, beliefs and harsh realities that he had been "fed." And yet, if you vomit, or "throw-up" (which he never does), out goes the only identity you have incorporated and you have nothing left: you are a non-person and risk drowning in a sea of ambiguity. This is a fate worse than death. Stossel writes: "I have sometimes been convinced that death, or something somehow worse, was imminent."

• • •

Prior to the Enlightenment, we knew life was difficult and looked forward to a utopian heaven. Quoting Hobbes from

"Leviathan" (1651), we knew life was "solitary, poor, nasty, brutish and short." But with the enlightenment breakthroughs in understanding and controlling nature (including our own), and the Industrial Revolution, came the idea of creating our own utopias here on earth. The idea of endless progress — religious and/or scientific — toward earthly utopias started there. As a counterpart to the surge in the expectation of happiness (the happiness myth), we came to deny the inherent tragedy of life. It's as though we decided that not only is life not tragic, but we are all happy here; if you don't agree we will label you anxious and depressed, and put you on medication so you won't raise embarrassing questions about our happiness myth. The worth of the individual even came to be evaluated largely in terms of his/her degree of support for, and ability to, enhance the happiness myth. Police attempt to prevent suicide.[6] The "tyranny of hope" is everywhere.

Opera used to be a popular celebration of the tragic life, but has now been sidelined by a public demand for optimism, spectacles of sex and violence, celebrities and blind euphoria. The human imagination and competitive spirit has served us well in creating the comforts of our civilizations. But it knows no limits; we imagine and demand utopias where we are all happy and important. Socialists predict utopias where we will all be important; everyone will be more important than anyone else. Could we take turns being important? History suggests that we define importance in relative terms; that we are only important if we "rise above the others" and we're never satisfied with the degree of difference. There is no satisfying the disease of celebrityitis.

• • •

Yeats' advice in 1891[7] that "we begin to live when we have conceived life as tragedy" comes as a shock to most people. They quickly dismiss the thought as not worthy of consideration. One piece in this puzzle is that it is easier to raise children when you promise them a happy life. Birthday parties, Santa Claus and the Easter Bunny are the symbols of great things to come. In the South, where I grew up, when a little girl hurt herself, the standard consolation used to be, "Don't worry honey, it'll be well before you get married." Many children even become saddled with the responsibility to support the parents' delusion of happiness; "children as antidepressants." Parents can be more dependent on their children than the children are on them (Phillips, *On Balance*, p. 98). We never recover from the failure to cure our parents.

This indoctrination with the expectation of happiness in children keeps them —when they later become adults — working hard with the naïve expectation that happiness is always just around the corner. Surely the next pay raise, or new car, or house, or spouse, or baby will finally bring the long awaited utopia and happy consolation. Like Charlie Brown and Lucy with the football, no matter how many deceptions ("good grief") are revealed, we seldom abandon that delusional trust in the future. It feels like the "only game in town." And there are at least two "good" things in that grief. Parents think of themselves as being good to their children when, by many subtle and indirect ways, they make happiness promises to their children. But they also make their own lives much easier (a "good" for them) because it is easier to raise optimistic children. Children are more cooperative when a utopian future is expected and/or they can anticipate power through prayer.[8] We turn a "blind eye" on how this makes the future of the children more problematic.

The second "good" for the parents is that children's "great expectations" also allow parents to nourish their beliefs in their own feelings of parental omnipotence and omniscience. Parents have even been known to prolong their children's feelings of inadequacy in order that the parents can perpetuate the feelings of power projected onto them by the children. The techniques employed by parents for this end are diverse, powerful, subtle and usually unconscious.

Some children and adults finally give up on the "football game" and become disillusioned and angry and begin to consider resignation and victimhood or rebellion. Those who choose resignation make good compliant workers who usually provide for their children and may experience some love. Victimhood is typified by narcissistic withdrawal and the search for reasons, such as diseases or discrimination, to be important. Those that choose rebellion are fair game for the military recruiters and/

or prisons. Yeats' suggestion that "we begin to live when we have conceived life as tragedy" advises us that we will only see the broader reality of life when we withdraw from the "football game." He did not mention that — although this perspective on life certainly opens up more possibilities for creativity and connections with others — disillusionment, despair, anger and social unrest may also accompany that broader attitude toward life.

Minority groups and lower classes are less susceptible to this happiness myth and less successful in "selling" this story to their children. The resulting social instability from refusing to play our "football game" produces things like jazz, (which I think of as music to accompany tragedies like funerals) and blues. Jazz and blues speak to us in consoling, but realistic, tones of tragedies we must live with; this is a reflection of the tragic but rich and multifaceted life outside the "football game." The happiness myth tends to restrict us to a one-dimensional life within which we must constantly struggle to defend our "happy-magic."

● ● ●

Although there were many wars before the Enlightenment, a significant part of our warfare and destruction of the planet today is explained by this denial of the general difficulty of life: our insignificance, the random tragedy and the paucity of joy and happiness compared with what we expect. Our anger increases in direct proportion to the discrepancy between what we have and what we expect from life. The sequence is: (1) Fear that our expectations are delusional, (2) Emotions of anger to displace the fear, (3) Search for a scapegoat on which to discharge the anger. Anger needs a scapegoat in order to prevent it from turning inward so we that we would "eat our hearts out." Warfare is the universal antidote, or at least outlet, for anger. There have been 3023 wars that we know of, but the evidence suggests there were more: that wars have been with us from the beginning; a hallmark of the species, perhaps. Ernest Becker gives another perspective in "The Denial of Death" (1973), to wit, when we deny our own death, as required by the happiness myth, it lives on in our unconscious and directs our lives from there causing much of the violence that takes place in the world.

We all feel ourselves in some sense to be important, and even God-like and immortal. So we struggle to confirm this conception, but we are such social animals that whatever significance we do achieve in society is always tenuous. We could lose it totally by some mistake (Governor Chris Christie and Lance Armstrong come to mind), or greatly enhance it tomorrow by some superhuman effort and/or a social fluke (Madam Curie and Charles Darwin). The "Horns of our Dilemma" are that being isolated from others, we can maintain our delusion of importance but lack the necessary confirmation from "accomplices." If, however, we pursue the life-affirming connection with others on anything more than a superficial level, we risk threats to our illusions and delusions of importance.

Hence, the frantic efforts to "nail down" our significance by garnering power, making lots of money, writing articles and books, and/or donating buildings with our names "carved in stone" — or written in graffiti, when we're poor. However, the significance is never enough; we always know at some level of consciousness that we are in fact insignificant and temporary and it terrifies, or at least unsettles, us. This tension keeps us busy creating new personal and social inventions and many complicated intrigues, both real and imagined. Scapegoats become essential to this mix so we can blame someone else for all of our troubles and then punish them as a catharsis for our fear and anger. Religious convictions are never complete, as in "Lord, I believe; help my unbelief." (Mark 9:24) Accordingly, we're often left with failed pleasure followed by greed and a need for scapegoats. Appetite can be satisfied; greed cannot: but warfare provides scapegoats and outlets for our anger.

These frantic efforts are justified and reinforced by the conviction in some future utopia as promised by our family, community and culture. The bad news is that, in fact, we are born between piss and shit, helpless, ignorant, scared and angry, just like all the other mammals; we spend the rest of our lives trying to deny it. We go to great lengths to prove how strong, smart and important we are; even to the extent of killing others. The blood will prove us right. We even once had a connection with a primary love-object that seemed to be loving, omnipotent and omniscient, but the belief and connection attenuated over time as we grew up then ended. We cannot accept that. It was not perfect but it was a part of our essential being and we want it back. "We live our lives forward but we desire backwards." (Phillips, *Intimacies*, p. 105). Hence, the prevalence of prohibitions against "looking backwards" in mythologies all over the world; Orpheus tries to rescue Eurydice from Hell but loses her when he "looks back." Lot's wife turns into a pillar of salt when she "looks back" at Sodom, to mention just two.

We are all "misbegotten," to use Eugene O'Neill's wonderful expression from his play, "A Moon for the Misbegotten." This is not the whole story, by any means, but it is important. We attempt to deny it so it comes back to "bite us in the ass" as a demon. That is, we start life, Phillips says, with a feeling that something is missing. But a large part of that "something missing" is the conviction that our self-consciousness is part and parcel of our centrality in the nature of things — even of the universe. And we have (had) omnipotent and omniscient parents who are totally devoted to us, and will always protect us from danger and disappointment. We feel there are innumerable pleasures in store for us in the future.

At some later point, we begin to perceive that these things are not true; that we are secondary in the importance of things and that, rather than pleasure, there is pain, tragedy and confusion always ahead. Thus we come to despair. We are misbegotten.

We come to feel that the best we can do subsequently is to create Gods and utopias as replacements, and strive and fight to make them real and attainable. We are born into a world without essential meaning, characterized by unpredictable tragedies and our own irrelevance. Intimate connections with other people over time, sharing some love and joy with others during good times, and bearing witness to the power and beauty of nature, all seem a poor substitute when we have such great expectations and fears at the same time. We attempt to bury our fears and seek consolation with "great expectations." We are indeed pitiful creatures. "We live, as we dream – alone."[9] How can anyone achieve a satisfying significance and consolation in such a setting? But this endless struggle seems to be the "only game in town." We feel that our only other option is to jump in the grave and let the human spirit die.

With this background of fear and desperation, it doesn't take much provocation and manipulation by leaders to identify a scapegoat who is the cause of all of this "Sturm und Drang." Then we can easily be convinced that with the elimination, or at least subjugation, of such evil people (how dare they interfere with my pursuit of happiness), we will finally achieve our utopia: the vaunted state of euphoria and permanent happiness. In part, this is the attempt to capture and replay the times in infancy that were joyful and peaceful. In the unconscious, those interludes happened yesterday. Or, as Adam Phillips says in "Going

Sane," pg. 159: "The sane adult is always smuggling his childhood into the future, refashioning his childhood pleasures as legitimate adult interests."

One of the "stepping stones" to understanding war is covered under the rubric of "cognitive capture." This term, first coined by William Buiter, is elaborated on by Chrystia Freeland in her 2012 book, "Plutocrats." It refers to the success of any group in imposing or "selling" their explanation of how the world works and how it should work. Fantasy is another stepping stone. All people operate on the basis of fantasy, albeit for the most part, the process is unconscious. It is usually some variation on "I am omnipotent and omniscient," like the parents were imagined to be; or at least, I deserve to be. We are more aware of beliefs that have their roots in those fantasies, such as our conviction that some people are evil and "out to get us," or at least interfering with our pursuit of utopia and the celebrity status we so "richly deserve."

Identifying these kinds of social processes helps to explain how we escape from the reality of our insignificant and haphazard lives and how dangerous this can be. We find ways to shut out harsh reality and live life within our comfort zones — our magical bubbles. Even war and possible death is preferable to the terrors of insignificance and other imagined perils.[10] Or, as Chris Hedges entitled one of his books: "War is a Force that Gives Us Meaning." We expect war to give life the meaning we want. It doesn't work out that way.[11] The interpretation of history, and wars in particular, varies widely depending on who is doing the writing and what types of formal and/or informal censorship and cognitive capture are operating. For instance, it is possible now to study Black history. Many veterans, the ones that did the fighting, are disillusioned, sick and angry.[12] Suicide among military personnel and veterans is an increasing problem. We always go to war, however, with the expectation it will give us the meaning we desire: Lucy and the "football" once again. Many historians have written about wars in such a way that they fit into our happiness myth. Tolstoy, Robinson, and especially Chris Hedges and Smedly Butler (who were closer to the scene) are more realistic. Once again, the real "enemy" is reality because it interferes with our pursuit of happiness, but without it our decisions will be flawed.

But we are always at war with reality, and with others, to secure some significance for our lives and to prove we are not as helpless, ignorant, scared and angry as we were when we were infants. Warfare adds physical violence to the usual psychological violence.[13] The worst tragedy resulting from this constant violence is that those of us lucky enough to succeed wrap ourselves so tightly in fantasies and narcissistic beliefs that we cannot let in — and thereby connect with — other people. This connection is the only true compensation for being human. This is the Hell of not being able to love. The compromise of letting in only pets and other sycophants who appear to worship us amounts to only so many bread crumbs when we desire and need a bakery. Because we are all wrapped in fantasies and beliefs designed to protect us from reality, we cannot see that we are killing ourselves and the planet that gives us life. Our desperate search for a utopian happiness — or, since that never works, scapegoats to punish — continues.

Add to this the many people whose disappointment and anger never gets converted into courage and positive channels. It simply spills over to killing ourselves along with everyone else around us, as in mass shootings, or in beliefs such as the annihilation of the earth and expectations of "rapture" or apocalypse. The various material "answers" — drugs, alcohol and religious forms of psychosocial numbing — amount to social cigarettes that afford temporary relief but lead inexorably toward the death of the human spirit and the planet.

Science doesn't provide us with guides on how to live life on an ethical basis. Nature has laws but no intentions or responsibilities (Phillips, *Darwin's Worms*, p. 16), (Mary Oliver, *The Kingfisher*). We unconsciously absorb the fantasies of inherent superiority and victimhood of those in our family and social class. In this respect, community fades in significance and the media gains in importance and power. The process continues across generations in a mostly unconscious way. If we become more aware of the fantasies, we realize that we must agree with and support those fantasies and beliefs or be an outcast; risk insanity and/or prison; be a non-person.

Early on, we sense that we risk punishment and death if

we challenge the fantasies and beliefs of those responsible for our care when we are infants and children; as we grow older, to challenge puts our jobs and livelihood at risk. We are more aware of certain beliefs supported by those fantasies than the actual fantasies; the beliefs guide our behavior. The usual fantasies are some variation of entitlement and superiority such as, "We are superior because we have a corner on God or science, beauty, wisdom or power." These fantasies support beliefs in future happiness based on the possession of wealth, popularity, love and sex; the things to which we feel entitled.

We may also feel we are victims because of past persecutions, or simply because we have to work so hard with unreasonable others and put up with servants who refuse to understand us. "It's just impossible to find good help these days." We should begin to extricate ourselves from this rather ludicrous trap we have made for ourselves and each other.

Science can often tell us what will happen if we live life in certain ways, which is a big help; but our beliefs, and their underlying fantasies, usually override scientific evidence, as is the case with climate change or the danger of drug interactions.[14] We always think we know the future better than the past, be it in terms of (1) an endless spiral of progress toward utopias, (2) a future to be shepherded in by an omnipotent, omniscient and beneficent God or (3) eminent apocalypse and annihilation by a wrathful God. They all relieve us of our painful responsibility of planning for a future dominated by rising sea levels, scarcities, overpopulation, chaos and more wars. That's one reason we're in so much trouble today.

Cognitive capture by secular or religious demagogues allows us to escape from science and reality, and provides us with more comfortable and taken-for-granted beliefs in what is in the future, and therefore acceptable in the present. Demagogues and Li'l Hitlers promise happiness and revenge, and get our money and votes. We now have numerous examples of tyrants and groups who captured the thinking of whole populations, and maintained control for a time through surveillance, censorship, violence and propaganda. We are much more sophisticated at manipulating public opinion than in the 1930's when Hollywood struck a deal with cigar-stand operators: we will show actors smoking cigars and you will put up posters advertising our movies on your cigar stands. Edward G. Robinson comes to mind. Product placement has a long history, but at least now we have a name for it. That's a start.

This malleability of the individual and culture is at once our curse and our blessing. It is a curse because powerful interests often seize large amounts of power, create a positive social image for their group by cognitive capture, and exploit society for the pursuit of their own happiness myth. In the extreme cases, these are always temporary. Protests, jail time, wars and revolutions result and we begin again. It is our blessing because these new beginnings provide opportunities to contribute something positive to the evolution of human societies; to examine the happiness myths and attempt better cultural responses to our existential anxiety. Slavery has been outlawed; women vote; education is more available…. but there are always battles raging quietly between vested interest groups where each struggles for a larger share of social resources. This is kept quiet to preserve the cognitive capture and social myth that "we're all happy here."

The work of propagandists, think tanks or social engineers is considerably simplified because they don't have to create something entirely new and get people to accept it; they only need convince them to morph existing beliefs into slightly different ones, often without modifying the underlying fantasies. The expectation of a return to the times of relative happiness and safety in infancy underlies many of the human fantasies and beliefs woven into our cultures.[15] When powerful people and demagogues, secular or religious, propose new and usually easy ways to achieve these goals, we are gullible; the old strategies didn't seem to work too well anyway. It is not as though we are anchored in some concrete reality and have to be pried out of it. We are more like freshly plowed ground waiting eagerly for some new seeds that will allow us to grow again and rise up into the hopeful sunshine of new fantasies — and thus not sink down into the dark, cold earth of reality and death.

We are all desperate for meaning and significance. Meaning that explains our existence and assigns us some significance within that explanation. Democracy can tolerate many varieties of these explanations but it does not provide them. Theocracy, plutocracy and fascism do. But because we live on fantasies, we are always a bit nervous about their efficacy. Conversions are frequent: we change or abandon religious or scientific beliefs, political parties, lovers, sexual preferences and personal identities. Most of us can be "reborn" into a new community or institution and network of beliefs with a minimum of effort. Fundamentalist and dominionist proselytizers know and exercise these techniques with precision, and promise a life free of difficulty if only you obey them (Chris Hedges, *American Fascists*). Action, violence and wars ("Onward Christian Soldiers") are sanctioned in these communities which also fuel the fires of apocalypse and disdain for future plans.

• • •

The "one percent" is also trapped in a make-believe cognitive framework like the rest of us. It's just different and, of course, self-serving with a large dose of entitlement. They plod along with a vision of happiness and how their entitlement and efforts will some day result in consolation of one kind or another. The economy should work just fine with light touch regulation, and if you're poor, it's your fault. Fair play and equal opportunity, formerly cornerstones of our culture and of Western Civilization since the Renaissance, are irrelevant. Even if these beliefs were "more honored in the breach," they were still more honored in the past. Greed and celebrityitis are rampant now, neither of which can be satisfied — only appetite can. There is a treatment for celebrityitis but no cure. The treatment requires a period of despair with the expectation that anger and courage will grow out of the despair sufficient to restore hope in the future through honest connections with others.

ENDNOTES

1   "There is a big secret about sex: most people don't like it." (Bersani and Phillips, *Intimacies*, 2008, p. 94.)

2   Donald Winnicott, *Hate in the Countertransference* lists 18 reasons for a mother to hate her baby.

3   Joseph Conrad in *Heart of Darkness* describes an almost pure manifestation of this "ego run rampant" in the character, Kurtz. Here the rampant delusional ego is combined with a talent for hypnosis — "the voice, the voice."

4   It could be argued that all humans have known love; that survival is impossible without it. But if the love of the parent(s) is only enough to provide physical survival, I would argue the child has never experienced true love.

5   Another perspective on suicide is provided by Adam Phillips: "Every suicide dispels the tyranny of hope," *Terrors and Experts*, p. 52.

6   From Yeat's autobiography; Book 1: *Four Years 1887-1891*. Also cited in *Reason's Grief* by George Harris, p. 18.

7   I recall asking my mother in my youth if it was true that if you prayed hard enough for something you would get it. She said 'yes,' and though I never tested the belief, it gave me great comfort.

8   *Heart of Darkness*, by Joseph Conrad: The Everyman Library, p. 32.

9   Among the many other perils is that if we return to the womb and dependence on Mommy, as a part of us is inclined to do, we also lose our autonomy, which we value greatly; big conflict.

10   The U.S. Civil War is a good example where both sides thought it would be a quick war with minimum casualties.

11   See "War is a Force that Gives Us Meaning" by Chris Hedges, and "Sparta" by Roxana Robinson, and "War and Peace" by Tolstoy.

12   Psychological violence was recently outlawed in France.

13   See "Premature Factulation" by Philip Hansten on the refusal of the medical profession to consider the dangers of some drug interactions.

14   There is a contradiction between our memory of infantile bliss and infantile terrors; but the unconscious has very little problem with accommodating to contradictions. There is even some harmony there as in "les extremes se touchent: or, the extremes touch.

CHAPTER 3

Life and Times of Frank Key

Returning now to the War of 1812, we were a fresh, new nation then, brash and arrogant; but we were also humiliated by the British impressments[1] (kidnappings) of American sailors for the Royal Navy and their burning of our nation's capital. We were caught by surprise when the British advanced on Washington, as our military felt Washington was not a strategic target. The British, however, attacked Washington in retaliation for our invasion of Canada the previous year, when we burned their capital, York, present day Toronto. After a short resistance at Bladensburg, Maryland, the hastily assembled American defense, mostly militia, broke and ran and abandoned the Capital to the advancing British. This was on August 24, 1814, and came to be known in the local papers as the "Bladensburg Races" in reference to the fleeing Americans. I must report that grandfather Key, a U.S. lieutenant in the militia at Bladensburg, was classified as a "sprinter" by local cartoonists and wits in that race to escape the enemy (Jefferson Morley, *Snow-Storm in August*, p. 53).

Key was opposed to that war as were many others — especially in the New England States. They felt negotiation could have prevailed, but Key enlisted in the militia more than once to defend his country during that war. On September 14, 1814, 21 days after the "races," he redeemed himself by successfully negotiating with the British on their ships, and securing the release of his friend, Doctor Beanes. It also provided the occasion on which he wrote the poem that became popular overnight, "The Star Spangled Banner." It had competition, however, for status as the national anthem. That didn't happen until 1931.

Eventually, we defeated the British in the War of 1812, or at least, it ended in a stalemate[2] and treaty which — considering the power of Great Britain and our virtual neophyte status as a nation — was a victory. After Napoleon abdicated in April 1814, many English troops and mercenaries became available and were sent to America to "dispatch" the troublesome colonials: three invasions were planned. However, much to the consternation of Britain, none were successful.

The first was launched from Canada, and the decisive battle — called both the Battle of Plattsburgh and the Battle of Lake Champlain— took place on Lake Champlain, just off Plattsburg, New York, from September 6 to 11, 1814. U.S. naval vessels decisively defeated the British ships. Superior British land forces, poised to invade Plattsburg, then retreated as there would be no way to resupply forces at Plattsburg while U.S. ships controlled Lake Champlain.

The second British invasion took place in the Chesapeake Bay area and focused on Washington City (the future D.C.) and Baltimore. They defeated Americans at Bladensburg, Maryland and burned public buildings in Washington, but were repulsed when attempting to capture Baltimore and spend the winter there.

The third and last invasion was aimed at New Orleans, which would have given them control of the Mississippi River trade route. The Treaty of Ghent, ending the war, had been signed and ratified by the English Parliament on December 27, 1814, but ironically, two American victories took place after that date (communication was slow; the first transatlantic telegraph cable would be completed in 1858). The first victory was at the Battle of New Orleans on January 8, 1815, where British troops were turned back in a land battle along the Mississippi River. The second was a naval battle off the coast of Spain on February 20, 1815, where the USS Constitution defeated two British ships: HMS Cyane and HMS Levant. Ultimately, Napoleon escaped from Elba on February 26, 1815, so Great Britain soon had another war to fight. There have been 3,023 wars. . .

General Andrew Jackson from Tennessee gets the credit for that U.S. victory in the State of Louisiana in 1815 (Louisiana Territory was purchased in 1803; Louisiana became a state in 1812). He gave part of the credit for that victory to Key, telling him the following story when they first met in Washington. While preparing for the Battle of New Orleans, he had read the words of "The Star Spangled Banner" and liked it so much, he distributed copies to his troops. He felt it improved their fighting morale. Jackson went on to become the 7th U.S. president (1829 – 1837) and Key was one of his allies in Washington.

• • •

Military victories demonstrate and inspire the confidence we long for: the fearless leader passes for the omnipotent and omniscient father and/or mother of our infantile memories. Also, contrary to our normal hectic lives, the enemies, goals and strategies are perceived as well defined and visible to all. It is one chaos that is subdued and clarified so we can understand it. There is a clear winner and a loser, and we long for those kinds of comforting dichotomies. Warfare simplifies history by defining it in terms of power or the lack of power.[3] Much of the normally mysterious and chaotic things in life are made manifest; although we (with the help of historians) downplay the very large part played by chance in victories and defeats, so we can hold on to this illusion of clarity. Uniforms, military parades and weapons — and, of course, flags — inspire confidence. But why should we need simplicity and confidence; why do we worry and doubt? Can we find no intrinsic meaning to life? Is there fear in the bosom of all? Is there uncertainty and terror always waiting in the wings? Is it true that "war is a force that gives us meaning"[4] and we are desperate for that meaning?

Another American victory in this war occurred on Lake Erie on September 10, 1813, when Commodore Perry defeated the British fleet there and sent his famous report: "We have met the enemy and they are ours." The other perspective on warfare was expressed succinctly by Walt Kelly's cartoon character, Pogo, in 1970: "We have met the enemy and he is us." Commodore Perry, roll over in your grave.

Key, an attorney in Washington in 1829, was repulsed by party politics. But when Jackson became president that year and nullification became an issue, Key did an about face and gave Jackson and the Democratic Party his ardent support. Nullification was the movement, spearheaded by South Carolina, that states had the right to "nullify," or ignore, any act of Congress that did not please them.

Among Key's political contributions was his defense of Sam Houston (Jackson's good friend) before the House of Representatives in 1832. Congressman William Stanbery from Ohio had accused Houston of corruption in a House debate, and it was published in a newspaper article. Houston, a six-foot-tall frontiersman in buckskin,[5] was so angry that he attacked Stanbery on a street in Washington and beat him with his hickory stick (Edward S. Delaplaine, *Francis Scott Key: Life and Times*, p. 326). Eventually, the House voted to censure Houston but Key's defense was days long and memorable. One point he made was that the stick Houston used in his attack was the same size with which, "in those strange old times," a husband was permitted to chastise his wife. Houston, formerly governor of Tennessee, had been wounded in the Indian Wars, and subsequently became President of the Republic of Texas. He was instrumental in bringing Texas into the Union in 1845: hence, Houston, Texas.

• • •

In 1833, during his second term in office, President Jackson nominated Key for U.S. District Attorney for Washington; Congress approved. He held that office for the next seven years until he retired. As well as handling difficult legal situations in Washington, Key was sent by Jackson to Alabama as a peacemaker in 1833 when conflict there escalated between Creek Indians, settlers on their land, state officials, U.S. Marshals and the U.S. military. The U.S. military had killed one illegal settler, and the state had attempted to arrest the military personnel involved. Key, now 54, shuttled back and forth for six weeks, negotiating with the governor, settlers, state officials and the U.S. military. He found compromises that all parties could agree to. He was a peacemaker, a poet and a devout Christian.

Key was active in the local Episcopal Church in Georgetown, where he lived. He was a lay reader, meaning that when the rector was unable to read the service (which was the case for many years), Key read the service and visited the sick and prisoners in jail. During this time, a mother came to him with a sick infant that she feared would die without being baptized; she asked Key to perform the baptism. Although not strictly qualified under church doctrine, he performed the baptism. He was then criticized for doing so by one Bishop Kemp. Key responded to the Bishop's rebuke: "You think it so clearly wrong that a moment's reflection 'ought to have arrested my progress.' I have reflected upon it since, and deliberately, and am still without any other reason for supposing it may be wrong than your telling me so. I hope, sir, you will excuse me for saying that this…. is not sufficient for me." (F.S. Key-Smith, *Francis Scott Key, a Kissinger Legacy Reprint*, p. 20.) Key considered becoming an Episcopal minister at one time but decided against it mainly because he wouldn't have been able to meet his financial obligations.

Key was also in Washington for the race riots of 1835 and prosecuted some of the participants on both sides of the issue. His own house was targeted for "ransacking" by the mob that accused him of being an abolitionist. Only the presence of armed guards prevented this. It says more about the mob's lack of toleration for ambiguity than Key's political stance. Key was known by some as the "black's lawyer" and had helped one James Hutton to secure his freedom by a letter to the court some ten years previously. (Jefferson Morley, *Snow-Storm in August*, p. 155.) But he owned slaves himself and believed freed slaves could not integrate into American society. He was a founding member (1817) and Vice President (until his death in 1843) of the American Bible Society which, along with the world-wide distribution of bibles, also promoted the strategy of colonization by blacks in Africa. In addition, Key was on the Board of Managers of the American Colonization Society, also founded in 1817, for the explicit purpose of raising money and arranging for the "return" of consenting freed slaves to Africa.

One of the many problems with this policy was that many, if not most, freed slaves had not been born in Africa, so could not be returned. Still, Key and many others worked toward that end for many years. The idea was to send freed slaves to a colony in Africa, later named Liberia, and founded for that purpose. It was "reasoned" they would be more at home and successful there. I think it's fair to say the issue of slavery tortured Key. He recognized it as a blight upon the land but, like a good peacemaker, he understood both sides of the argument. Today we describe this policy as an attempt to exploit slaves and then dispose of them by shipping them back to Africa. Our current version of this is when employers have their illegal migrant workers arrested and returned to their countries of origin, often without the benefit of wages earned. Colonization was a misguided but popular policy. It was, at least, based on the logic of the time, the current cognitive capture, rather than fear, anger and violence.

Contributing to the race riots of 1835 was a slave revolt in 1831. Fifty-five white Virginians were massacred during Nat Turner's rebellion (William Styron, *Confessions of Nat Turner*). This produced fear, anger and reprisals in many of the slave states. Key's response was to allow his "head slave" on the family estate of Terra Rubra in North-Central Maryland, to buy his freedom for $5; Key then hired him back to work for wages. He permitted his one resentful slave to buy his freedom for $300 and leave, thus eliminating a "trouble maker." This was how he maintained control over the seven remaining adult slaves, and promoted peace at home. The slaves at Terra Rubra (a.k.a. Pipe Creek) were encouraged to meet every day at sundown for Christian prayers. This rearrangement of slaves could be called Machiavellian, but at least it was diplomatic, not violent. Michael Ignatieff has some good things to say about Machiavelli in the December 2013 The Atlantic Magazine. It is a good example of Key's skill as a peacemaker. In many southern states, new repressive laws were passed to further restrict the freedom of slaves. Some fear makes us more aware of our environment or, as Samuel Johnson put it, "When a man knows he is to be hanged in a fortnight, it concentrates his mind wonderfully." Too much fear paralyzes or panics; anger motivates: perhaps that has something to do with the 3,023 wars.[6]

• • •

We made peace with the British, rebuilt the capital and continued to expand our boundaries westward. We populated the land: Key had 11 children; his daughter Elizabeth had 10; his granddaughter Mary, 8 (one of whom was my maternal grandfather). We welcomed waves of immigrants to our shores, created farms, factories and stores, and built schools, hospitals, churches, roads and railroads. In the process, we also mistreated many of our slaves, our poor, our native Indians and Mexicans. We killed 90% of the native Indian population just with our diseases; sometimes deliberately.

We followed our "Manifest Destiny," that magical-religious justification for successful imperialism. There are six monuments to Key: five are in the Maryland/D.C. area but there is a very impressive one in Golden Gate Park, San Francisco, built in 1888. It was the first memorial to Key, and the funding came from the bequest of an individual. It could symbolize the completion of our conquest of the continent as well as our opportunity to look further westward. We felt impelled to bring Christianity and the work ethic, enlightenment and prosperity to others such as Alaskans, Hawaiians, Filipinos and Japanese. James Bradley examines this epoch in his book "Imperial Cruise." Perhaps it is time now — 200 years after the battles of 1814 and with the nation and the world once again (or still) in dangerous turmoil — to try to understand our deeply buried fear, anger and confusion. Do we create delusions like Manifest Destiny and racism in response to those feelings? Do we go to war partly in order to give meaning to a life devoid of any intrinsic meaning? Even if it takes another 200 years, we need to address and eventually understand and control these dynamics. Why have we had 3,023 wars? Perhaps it is time for the exploration of our "inner spaces." Perhaps we can still save our civilization and our planet, or at least prolong the existence of our species.

ENDNOTES

1   The British argued that they had a right to seize British sailors from American ships; that those born in Britain were British for life. Irvin Molotsky, in "The Flag, the Poet and the Song," suggests that possibly 25% of the 50,000 to 100,000 American sailors in the early 19th century were in fact British who had deserted from the navy or jumped ship from merchant vessels because the American ships offered a better life.

2   Some of the British considered the war more as a punitive expedition than a war of conquest. It was punishment for the upstart Americans who had the audacity to declare war on Great Britain. At any rate, it got their attention: the new American nation was not to be trifled with.

3   Just so, many insecure people define their relations with others in terms of power in order to impose meaning on a life that is basically incomprehensible. They miss out on all of the intriguing mysteries and subtleties of human relations and intimacy.

4   The title of a book by Chris Hedges.

5   Houston was so poor at the time that he couldn't afford to buy

the style of clothing expected in the Capital. As he said in his testimony before the House, "the ploughshare of ruin has been driving over me ..." (Delaplaine; *FSK* p. 340). Andrew Jackson called him into the White House and gave him money to buy new clothes for the remainder of his trial. Houston was also called "The Raven" as he was so named by the Cherokee Indians when he had been adopted and lived with them for more than a year as a young man, and later in life at times of adversity. In the attack on Stanbery, Houston probably would have been killed by Stanbery's pistol had it not misfired.

6   How many soldiers never fire a shot in a battle? Fear paralyzes; it's best if they hate the enemy; hate will pull the trigger. Then we're surprised at war crimes and atrocities. How much of Post-traumatic stress disorder (PTSD) is the struggle to put the "genie (the rampant ego) back in the bottle?" See Chapter 2 "Killing" (p. 32) and Indian War Dance (p. 37) of "This Republic of Suffering" by Drew Gilpin Faust.

CHAPTER 4

Illusions and Delusions That Give Life Meaning

Such a shift in emphasis to inner space seems called for by the impasse, turmoil and violence (physical and psychological) in Washington, Wall Street and elsewhere around our country and the world. We seem to feel that the "stakes in the competition game" are much higher than they really are.

We have "chilling thoughts" about our significance; we seem to fear some fate worse than death, like complete annihilation of our life and even any memory of our life, if we don't succeed in our struggles. We seem to fear "that death, or something somehow worse, [is] imminent." And many do die physically of greed and anger, while still striving for some obscure and impossible goal that "gives life meaning." While we all have the goal of self-preservation, we are also driven by "suicidal self-love," the ultimately self-destructive will to master the world," (Leo Bersani and Adam Phillips, *Intimacies*, p. 103).

Much of the population of the world is not even in this international "game." They do, however, get to exercise tyranny and incest within families and die a "social death," i.e., disappear from (or never appear on) the "registry of who is important." This includes all the occupants of all the "skid rows" and ghettos around the world.

Key takes note of this universal fear in a speech he gave at the celebration of George Washington's birthday in February 1814, saying that he trusted that Washington never felt the "chilling thought" that his name would be forgotten or disregarded (Washington died in 1799). Much of social structure is about putting limits on the ways we can go about avoiding that chilling thought. Celebrityitis is only the latest product of that dynamic. We attempt to define whole segments of populations as "nobodies," as not entitled to pursue the goal of social immortality while still proclaiming equality for all. We fight like wild dogs over the right to be remembered, but to what ends? We are all destined for blank oblivion ultimately, but seem to fear we will be incapable of functioning as humans if we accept that. This is the great draw of Christian religions: fundamentalists, dominionists and the prosperity gospel messages in particular ("You will be a Christian celebrity now, or at least in heaven"). But all of our goals are at best unclear: atheists, agnostics and religionists alike. All "important groups" seem motivated primarily by the attempt to "expand the ego" (Bersani, p. 55) in order to avoid the chilling thoughts of insignificance that go with contemplating reality.

Warfare is just one very clear example of this continuing bizarre struggle. Are we that ignorant of human nature or do we exploit human nature and make up publicly acceptable reasons for the wars? Is it really our unconscious that's in control and we have no clue as to why we do what we do? Is it saber rattling that gets out of control? Why do we feel impelled to rattle our sabers in the first place? Is there a human destructiveness inside each of us that craves violence and death; even our own? Does the mere existence of another person, who seems more satisfied with life than we are, threaten our own precarious argument for self-importance? Are we all involved in a bitter contest to pretend we are more satisfied than anyone else? Or at least, we admire idols that are more satisfied/beautiful/powerful than anyone else.

• • •

Sharing of political and economic power in the U.S. has always been contentious. The nation was seriously divided about declaring war on Britain in 1812. But now we appear to have reached the brink of a new power-tragedy. Most of the wealthy (here and world-wide) seem desperate and greedy to accumulate more wealth and power to stave off increasing doubts that money will deliver on their delusions of satisfaction. They want consolation, freedom from frustration and, of course, happiness. Power over other people is real but power interferes with happiness just as wealth does. Our greatest joy in life, though we can't recognize it because we are greedy and desperate for something more, comes through our connections with others (Bersani and Phillips, *Intimacies*, and *Vaillant, Triumphs of Experience*). We are social animals. Peace of mind, to the extent possible, must be rooted in self-understanding and tolerance of the turmoil and uncertainty deep inside us and others. Happiness is love (more on this later).

There is a kind of continuous rebirthing possible; but it is painful. Without power or wealth we can experience despair. While counterintuitive, this gives us the opportunity to search within ourselves, our family and friendships; to search within community, history and our future for something approaching reciprocity — the sharing of the mystery of life and perhaps even love. Auguste Rodin's sculpture, "The Prodigal Son," (on the cover of this book) captures the painful quandary of young and old. But within that very despairing lie the seeds for growth into maturity as with the prodigal son.[1] He is wrestling with reality and so may create a more meaningful life for the future. When we have power and wealth, there is always some new expensive technique and/or product which promises easy ways to find and keep happiness.

Despair is like a self-shattering, be it the despair that accompanies personal random tragedy or like the prodigal son who sees he cannot make it on his own. Even the let-down accompanying orgasm, when we realize our magical expectations have vanished and we are all alone, has some of this despairing flavor.[2] But from this fresh start, this self-shattering — painful and even terrifying as it may be — we at least have a better chance to reassemble our expectations and consequent strategies in a more realistic fashion. The shattering and despair is always terrifying, regardless of how many times we experience it. This is because we're never confident that we can put ourselves back together again, or even more risky, reassemble ourselves into a more effective being.

And the terror is well founded. We can never be certain we will "come back" in any familiar or useful form. We may sink into psychological and social oblivion… never come back. Our fear is out of proportion to the risk involved, but no less terrifying for our unconscious deals in possibilities, not probabilities. There is the possibility of a psychotic break.

So, like Charlie Brown and Lucy with the football, and regardless of all the previous missed balls and "good griefs," the rich and powerful are compelled to try another external "solution," which leaves that inner cauldron of fear, anger, greed and emotional conflict untouched. Balance is a key word here: too much despair leads to depression and death of one kind or another. The desperate at all levels of society need company. Not the kind of company that promises a cure or escape through compassion, religion or drugs, but rather friends who will share the desperate feelings, legitimize the despair and encourage connections with other people and creative approaches to life, rather than a retreat into greater delusions and idols of one kind or another (Chris Hedges, *Losing Moses*, pp. 51, 75, 92, 117, 165). We are all, in a sense, "abandoned children" and "despairing adolescents." We have a lot of "bullet-biting" to do. "Focusing" provides one pathway toward these more significant connections with others; and it's virtually free (see Focusing.org).

• • •

The road to despair, however, is paved with fear, anger, confusion and magic. Most of us succumb to the temptation of fixating on some magical formula of anger and power as the way to cover over the fear, despair and confusion, and to motivate the struggle to be. The hope, like Charlie Brown, of achieving our delusions of happiness "springs eternal in the breast of humans." Joining gangs, corporations, the military or political parties (institutional loyalty), offers access to support and shares the fear, anger, and scapegoats with like-minded others. The more people (accomplices) that agree on the magic and the more blood (literal or figurative) that flows, the stronger it feels — the more real. Hence, the ceremony of communion in Christian churches includes the symbolic drinking of Christ's blood because it makes our delusional perception of life feel more real. "Cutters" self-mutilate for the reassuring sight and taste of their own blood. Ritualized blood-letting such as sacrifices to Gods, and Japanese eating the livers of American airman (James Bradley, *Fly Boys*) testify to the enduring importance of ritualized blood-letting, drinking the blood and eating the flesh of others in order to increase belief in fantasies.

So we stumble along "making do" with blood and institutional loyalty — violent sports, road-kills and "the emperor has beautiful clothes." But you risk banishment if you question the magic of the blood or institutions. Key was exceptional when he questioned the magic of his Bishop: the blood of communion and the institution of the church.

As a backdrop to much of this fantasy-upkeep, it seems we live in a constant state of anticipation, where we can almost taste some ultimate power and satisfaction just around the corner of our life's trajectory. Like the celebrities we admire so much, we can feel ourselves celebrating and starring in our own movie, safe from the threat of crowds who ignore us. Despair is mostly an unknown category that suggests weakness; it is as frightening as death itself for it is a kind of dying: letting die the delusions of ultimate happiness and power with their roots deep in our infancy.[3]

In response to these desperate difficulties, we have invented a plethora of cultural diversions in order to mask our fear, anger, confusion and anxiety, and avoid despair. Lives are organized into loud, quick "sound bites" so there is no opportunity for contemplation and despair. Blaise Pascal wrote, in the 17th century, that "All men's miseries derive from not being able to sit in a quiet room alone." We have learned to distinguish cause and effect better now, but it is still in large part true that we create a lot of our miseries — war included — from not being able to "bite the bullet" of silence and despair.

Again, Yeats speaks eloquently to this issue: "We begin to live when we have conceived life as tragedy." As long as we spend our energy and attention on striving to avoid and deny tragedy and despair, and attempting to create magical safety, power, meaning and satisfaction, we will miss out. We will miss out on the other more realistic opportunities for satisfaction by way of creative despair and intimate connections with other people. As long as we keep denying the inevitable tragic aspects of life, like the fact that our infantile hopes are futile and no being is omnipotent and omniscient, we will not begin the creative cycles of despair, creativity, new connections with others and new hope that lead to better plans for the future.[4] If we continue what may be the most profound 'mistake' inherent in being human: that of preferring our opposition to the world we live in over our correspondence, "our friendly accord," with it,"[5] we will miss out on the best part of being human.

We can, in a sense be "reborn." Despair, bordering on depression, is the main source from which our creative and peace-making juices flow. It provides us with the possibility of reassessing the present and our place in the world, and helps us to visualize alternate approaches to future problems. "Those who cannot remember the past are condemned to repeat it;" "Good Grief" (George Santayana and Charlie Brown). We need, from time to time, to "sit in a quiet room alone" — to meditate.

But still, we seem to feel we know the future better than the past. Despair was a large part of the life of that devout Christian, Frank Key. Perhaps the experience and acceptance of despair is more important than the particular framework within which it is couched, i.e., Key's Christian framework has similarities with that of other religions, and with some secular humanist philosophies. If God is omnipotent and beneficent, why is there so much suffering?[6] Key seems to have used religion not to escape from despair, but rather as a kind of container for the idea and feeling of despair.

Most people let tragedy control their lives. To the extent we devote resources to avoiding tragedy, it is in the driver's seat; it controls our lives. It is only when we can accept that tragedies are inevitable and unpredictable that we can then be open to the joyful possibilities of our lives in between the tragedies. Accepting tragedy opens up a whole new perspective on life. It is counterintuitive but the only way to "win" with tragedy is to accept it. Key seems to do this with a religious perspective: "All things are God's will." Thus, tragedy is God's will and we must accept it. Key is allowed to stop fighting against tragedy, to accept it along with the creative despair, and then enjoy the "blessings" in between.

Another trap we fall into is expecting life to make sense: we would like to eliminate confusion. Phillips puts it succinctly: "The ego's project is plausibility," (*Intimacies*, p. 92). Indeed, the book you are reading is the result of my search for plausibility. We are a "sense-making species" and it has served us well in terms of learning to control and exploit the physical and natural world around us. But we expect similar results when we desire to understand random tragedies, why we exist in the first place and where we are going next, if anywhere. I would modify the Yeats' quote thus: "We begin to live better when we have conceived of life as tragedy and learned to tolerate and even celebrate life as a mysterious tragedy." Otherwise, we tend to search for some proximate or ultimate explanation for random tragedies — and life in general — usually couched in terms of religion, magic and scapegoats when the evidence suggests there is none.[7] Thus, illusions of exorbitant self-importance, including celebrity status and an exaggerated sense of the value of money and power, flourish in our world. This interferes with intimate connections with other people and the problem-solving we so desperately need in order to avoid future chaos and wars.

• • •

Many seem to live life as though they were stars in their

own movie, including fundamentalist preachers. I'm labeling this as celebrityitis; a plague of celebrityitis. Sue Bloland describes the way her famous father, Eric Erickson, would walk into a restaurant and just by his demeanor, people would assume he was someone famous, (Susan Bloland, *In the Shadow of Fame*, p. 1).

In a similar vein, we come up with religious-magical explanations for things that have no explanation, but they help to "sell the product" or benefit group cohesion: "God in three persons" or the "evil witches" executed in Salem, Massachusetts (19) or Europe (35,000). Traditional witch-hunts and the actual killing of "witches" continue today in New Guinea, India and Africa. I might be identified as "un-American" or a witch because of my lack of commitment to shared values and magical beliefs of my time. I thereby threaten the relative equanimity of the group, which is always based in part on magical beliefs (we're better than others; they have it all wrong). The loss of one community member, one black magic witch, is less important than affirming and preserving the consensus about the efficacy of the group's "white magic" through blood and violence. Sacrifice of animals is at least a step away from war.

Pretending to be a star without sufficient community support can be dangerous. Perhaps Jesus Christ was a sensitive schizophrenic with celebrityitis, who felt how desperate we were for consolation and so hallucinated a comforting story for him and us. But he lacked a sufficient quota of community support and so he was classified and crucified as just another witch. Subsequent church fathers added to the story and created much wisdom in their struggles with despair. Can we face the truth enough to rescue the planet and our species from premature death?

ENDNOTES

1   This sculpture has been exhibited under various titles: "Despairing Adolescent;" "The Child of the Century;" "Vae Victis;" and "The Warrior." It also appears in the right-hand panel of the "Gates of Hell." Jean-Baptiste Carpeaux created an earlier version of despair titled "Despair" which may have influenced Rodin plus Carpeaux's "Ugolino and Sons" and his concentration on shipwrecks illustrate family and group despair.

2   This is one reason why Bersani and Phillips believe "most people don't like sex," 2008, p. 94. It sometimes makes a mockery of our passion to rule the world and unleashes a countering violence.

3   Chris Hedges cites the case of Raskolnikov in *Crime and Punishment* by Dostoyevsky on p. 165 of *Losing Moses*: "He murdered because he was afraid he would not be extraordinary. He was afraid that one day he would vanish and never leave his mark."

4   Alfred Lord Tennyson comes to mind among so many who created great cultural gifts out of their despair.

5   Leo Bersani and Adam Phillips, *Intimacies*, (p. 125)

6   This is the problem of theodicy; highlighted by the slaughter of 600,000 in the U.S. Civil War who all believed in the same God (see p. 188 of *This Republic of Suffering* by Drew Gilpin Faust).

7   George Harris explores the philosophical underpinnings for this "making sense" dilemma in *Reason's Grief* and cites the

Yeats quote about tragedy, (p. 18).

CHAPTER 5

Recapturing Infancy

Many of us are like crying infants who expect to avoid all frustration and have all our wishes gratified, "immediately if not sooner." We are all vulnerable to regression, to the madness of infancy, in times of stress. And even increasing wealth is stressful, partly because it brings a new identity but also because it fails to deliver on expectations — and even creates guilt. Remember the anxiety experienced the first time you rode in the first class cabin of an airplane?[1] Magnify that by 1000 for the nouveau riche or the newly poor. Or think of the failed dinner party of the "Unsinkable Molly Brown." We even have a diagnosis now: "Sudden Wealth Syndrome," and at least one clinic in California where you can go for treatment. The usual symptoms are feeling isolated from former friends, guilt over the good fortune; and fear of losing all the money. The treatment is to create an exaggerated sense of entitlement. A study at an intersection in Los Angeles revealed that the more expensive the car, the more likely it was to deprive pedestrians or other cars of the right-of-way.

I suspect that if and when we delve deeper into this syndrome, we will find that because our sense of "ego expansion" is so flexible (Leo Bersani and Adam Phillips, *Intimacies*. p. 55), sudden wealth brings home to us that if we can "expand" infinitely, we can also "contract" infinitely. And that if we contract far enough, we cease to exist in time; we were never here. This will "fire-up" your fear (everyone has it) of non-existence. For people with a consistent sense of their worth over time, this is not so much of a problem. But a rise or fall in self-worth represents a collision with the virtual quality of identity: it can slide anywhere, either up, down, around or sideways. Once again, we are social animals. We need one another in order to anchor our identities.

We feel we know the future better than the past, regardless of disappointments, failures and predictions of disasters that came true. We cannot give up the hope of a return to infantile experiences. Our memory seems to operate on an automatic discard of unpleasant occasions and failures, and perhaps this has an advantage: while we may continue to make the same mistakes over and over, at least we are not paralyzed by fear. Even the much touted and longed-for status of wealth is often a disappointment. We may even find that a new position of wealth once achieved requires a pretense of happiness in order to create envy in others and secure the new social status... to be accepted into the "let's pretend club" ... to share power. Adam Phillips suggests that the idea of the "good life" has now been replaced by the "enviable life" (*On Flirtation*, pp. 58, 135).

The main purpose of all religion, drugs, alcohol and entertainment is to recreate and perpetuate the infant's feeling of omnipotence and omniscience in self and in caretakers so we can escape — or at least mitigate temporarily — our "quiet [or not so quiet] desperation." This is seldom an either/or commitment, but rather like a vacation into a realm we know is part fiction but where we can still experience some consolation. God in three persons is us: mother and father and me, wrapped in love and harmony together.

It seems that we struggled to achieve personal and social advantages (mostly material) in the 19th century with the expectation that they would bring the much-vaunted (mostly by Madison Avenue but couched in the pursuit of utopias in general) consolation. When the desired social and personal level of living was achieved and consolation was still absent, we became desperate and greedy. We needed a new "answer" for our existential anxiety. The "good life" was not good enough. Hence was born the rough outlines of the enviable life as the new panacea. That was more practical: a life that would be envied by others and thus make us feel powerful and important. "Greed is despair about pleasure" (Adam Phillips, *On Kissing, Tickling and*

Being Bored, p. xix). But the "enviable life" is a consolation prize and — like all consolation prizes — is tinged with bitterness, anger and resentment and therefore in need of scapegoats. There is no thought here of virtue, ethical behavior or love; it is all about making others envy you regardless of the source of wealth or power. It's about being a celebrity. Greed replaces the despair, whereas if we can "ride-out" the despair, it may take us to a new place.

The great expectations of infancy are difficult to outgrow, especially when encouraged by parents desperate to be perceived as powerful and wise by their children. We may repress these infantile expectations but this madness is always there "waiting in the wings" to come to our "rescue." This tendency seems to combine with a current "hubris of appetite" in our culture to produce some of our megalomaniac tendencies and personalities. On the other extreme, many feel they are trapped between rising expectations and diminishing opportunities even for low-paying jobs.

The old ploy of providing and humiliating scapegoats in the media, such as the ungodly or wrong-godly, immigrants (legal or otherwise), racial stereotypes, sexual "deviants," Muslims and — the newest — big government, can provide only limited relief. Of course, when all else fails, we can always go to war; this is a "sure-fire" way to divert people's attention away from looming despair, unfair social policies, fear and confusion. But the frustration among upper and lower classes continues to mount as we pursue chimeras of consolation and happiness. It is worth remembering Freud's words on the last page of "Civilization and Its Discontents," that we all demand consolation, "the wildest revolutionaries no less passionately than the most virtuous believers." And I would add, the rich no less than the poor. Freud concluded: "I bow to [their] reproach that I can offer no consolation."

• • •

Being human means being anxious and all human behavior is preceded by frustration: the minor frustration of whether or not and when to get out of bed in the morning, or the more general and threatening frustration of "to be or not to be." "… The child's dawning awareness of himself is an awareness of something necessary not being there," (Adam Phillips, *Missing Out*, p. xix). Granted, with advancing age and resignation, frustration may become an accustomed companion. Crying babies are more aware. Frustration precedes every human action. The frustration is what motivates us. Michael Eigen suggests there is an optimum level of frustration required at any given moment in order for us to feel psychologically alive (1993:34).

Frustration fuels the drug economy because we can imagine a life free of frustration. It ain't going to happen! I imagine a frustration-free life inside the womb where eating, breathing and pissing were taken care of automatically and there was no shit. But it must have become cramped after a while; perhaps I was startled by loud noises or abrupt movements beyond my control. My sleep was disturbed: thus it begins. Pornography is largely an attempt to recapture the union with mother's naked breast and the return to mother's womb; the once and only "heaven" and true merger with another that we will ever know. The unconscious is not fussy about sequences and we feel we were there "yesterday." When frustration leads to impossible desires, our frustration reaches a fever pitch; anger and violence often ensue. Small wonder we're frustrated, angry and confused; we had that "heaven" once; why can't we have it back again? In the unconscious, it was yesterday. Again, "we live, as we dream – alone."

Our anxiety and confusion is also frustrating. Anxiety, the existential anxiety that goes with being human, makes people jump to conclusions. Delay means more anxiety and frustration. We yearn for powerful, smart leaders who exude confidence by making snap decisions and giving easy answers we can comprehend. They seem to diminish confusion. It is a bad time on our planet for spurious omniscience. Leaders who take time and tolerate the ambiguity of confusion and not knowing are more apt to come up with the best available answers and even better questions. We need to "bite the reality bullet"! All humans need things life cannot provide; not even if we're willing to wait forever, and work forever and accumulate unlimited wealth and power. There are even more things that we want and can't have. The disparity between what we need and want and what we can actually achieve — regardless of power and wealth — is a great wound in the human psyche and fosters a need for revenge and/or self-punishment.

So how did we come up with the idea in the first place that we should be happy? Was it "Happy celebrities?" Madison Avenue? The medical/pharmaceutical industry? These promises of happiness rub salt in the wounds inflicted by the disparity between what we want and what we can have. Sadly, many go mad and/or die struggling for something that is impossible, a delusion. One thing we all yearn for deep down in the unconscious is the womb-like merger and "heaven" with mother, which brings safety, rebirth and hence, immortality. We also grasp unconsciously for the return and achievement of our infantile fantasy of omnipotence and omniscience. We deny life's "difficulty" by our conviction we can be happy (our optimism is dangerous). Our initial perception of our caregivers is just that: they are omnipotent and omniscient, partly because we perceive what we want to perceive. It makes us feel safer. And, responding to that need in the infant, the parents are usually willing to assume an attitude of absolute power and knowledge. It may be one of their few satisfactions in life. Children that feel safe are easier to raise and parents can experience the pleasure of pretending to be omnipotent and omniscient (for a change). A win/win... for a while. This leads, however, to the infant's expectation that they can also achieve unlimited power at some time and in some way. We feel that ideal mergers and absolute power would make us happy! The unconscious has no problem with contradictions and since these things are impossible, they will always be there to tantalize us.

It's not going to happen, folks! And instead of happiness, we endure a painful birth between piss and shit, all of us, and this just the prelude to other tragedies and traumas of greater magnitude. That is, as Ernest Becker points out, even though we experience ourselves down deep as magically gifted immortals at the center of the universe, we are in fact insignificant animals destined for death and blank oblivion — when, where and how, we know not. "My desire may be in excess of any object's capacity to satisfy it, but I am not going to begin by believing this." (*Intimacies*, p. 104.)

We were born between piss and shit and, at the same time, evicted from our once and only "heaven." This happens in spite of trying to possess and marry mommy or daddy (in any of its multiple unconscious forms); owning guns; joining gangs, fraternities, religions and political parties; military camaraderie and victories; marriage contracts; partnership deals; fame, fortune and celebrity status. Perhaps even murder (if murder is a penetration and merger with the body of another), and psychological violence (if that's a penetration and merger with the mind of the other), reflect our frantic attempts at intimacy, power and merger. We are basically alone since birth — helpless, ignorant, scared, angry and destined for blank oblivion.[2]

No wonder we are desperate for power and make wars that will provide an outlet for our anger and prove our power to the world! We seem incapable of accepting our animal nature and brief existence, and instead invent other reasons for our grief. These reasons can be addressed, like more money and power, blaming other people and countries and religions that are somehow responsible and need to be punished.[3] With this essential nature of the human condition, it is easy to see why all religions have such a difficult time implementing policies of love and peace to communities and nations and even their own organizations.

Even Key, devout Christian, poet and expert negotiator, was unable to prevent "war" within his own family. Four of his sons died violent and tragic deaths; one drowned and two were shot to death. A fourth died of disease in 1837 at age 29. Our species seems incapable of reconciling our feeling of personal importance with that ultimate random tragedy, insignificance and blank oblivion. When we experience that "chilling thought" of being forgotten, we rattle our sabers and draw our swords and sometimes go to war like an infant with a temper tantrum. Key's son Daniel must have felt something of that when he argued with a fellow midshipman; he eventually challenged him to a dual and was killed at age 20. "War" in the family continued after Key's death: his son Phillip Barton was shot to death by Daniel Sickles, the irate husband of his lover.[4] Phillip was 40 and left four children. It is safe to say the irate husband felt "forgotten" and diminished, and responded accordingly. Phillip was reportedly the most handsome widower in Washington and could have partnered with any number of other women. I suggest he "fell in love" with a married women because, unconsciously, she resembled his mother in the sense that she was married to a father figure. He was already a widower so his four children were left without a mother or father.

Considering the origins of the human species for a moment, our insecurity and necessity for social support, affirmation and our resulting team cooperation may account for our dominance over predators and Neanderthals and other rival species on the Earth. The other humanoids may have been more like cats (lions excepted) — independent creatures — while we were more like dogs with their pack instinct. Perhaps our constant strivings for social recognition and superiority, along with leading to war and other forms of violence, are also the seeds for our unceasing creativity and productivity. If this is the case, it would be a distinct advantage for our species but a curse for the individual.

ENDNOTES

1 Or, if you grew up flying first class, then your first occasion in tourist class.

2 Blank oblivion is not necessarily a negative term. It comes from a poem by John Clare: "and blank oblivion reigns as earth's sublime." (Quoted in *On Flirtation* by Adam Phillips, p. 217).

3   John Steinbeck in *Travels with Charlie* (1962), found that poultry farmers in New England found a way to blame Russia and the Communists when egg production was down.

4   Sickles successful defense at his trial utilized "temporary insanity" for the first time.

CHAPTER 6

Fear

Fear plagues us all! It comes in many shapes and sizes and degrees of awareness and sources. Nightmares give the lie to those who would deny all fears. The basic template for fear is perhaps the birth trauma. We were secure once and then, like Humpty Dumpty on the wall, it all came tumbling down, and "All the king's horses and all the king's men, couldn't put Humpty together again." The fear is replayed in the story of Adam and Eve being cast out of Paradise. The basic fear reflected in these stories is that it doesn't matter how safe you feel, it may end abruptly; you can never "rest on your laurels," you must always be afraid.

A second paradigm for fear comes later on when we discover that caregivers are not omnipotent and omniscient; they cannot always protect us and sometimes don't even care about us. With luck, we live for a time with the comforting illusion that it is true, that we are safe and this provides some optimism toward life. Without luck, childhood diseases and/or displacements or other tragedies intrude on the illusion, and we must face tragedies sooner in life and our outlook on life will be soured. Wealthy families with better access to comforts and security can usually prolong the feeling of trust longer. They can produce more optimistic children, many of whom feel "entitled" to a life-time of comforts designed to allay the basic fears. It works, though, only as a distraction — the basic demons, the fears of "ejection," ultimate death and insignificance are always with us.

Perhaps the larger problem is what to do with the fear when we do begin to see that "light;" when we do begin to accept some of the tragic dimensions of life and the accompanying uncertainty and fear. Fear in small doses is a good thing: "It wonderfully concentrates the mind," as Samuel Johnson said. Fear makes us more aware of our environment, more sensitive to others we come in contact with. When we have too little fear, we are naïve and may even have a manic defense such that we exclude fear from awareness. But too much fear may paralyze with paranoia and/or lead to escape attempts by way of comforting myths or psychosis or drug/alcohol addiction. Anger motivates. It will cover over the fear. Who can we blame? "There must be someone I can focus my anger on and humiliate or murder! I feel I will explode or go crazy otherwise! Let's go to war!" THREE THOUSAND OF THEM.

Christianity used to provide a "container" or structure for much of the fear and accompanying anger: Islam still does (perhaps because it is 700 years younger). In the Middle Ages, we could hate and go to war against non-believers with the magical expectation that once everyone is killed or converted, and/or the Messiah returns, the expected infantile and/or womb-paradise would finally be ours. Bernard de Clairvaux rebuked the King of France for killing 1,300 French people by burning down the church at Vitry where they had taken refuge. He recommended the Second Crusade as penance. Pope Urban II (for the First Crusade): "If you must have blood, bathe your hands in the blood of Infidels." Today religious violence is not only physical (like murder and cutting the hair of rivals) but also psychological with humiliation often the weapon of choice.

Our current uncertainties and confusions are fueled by a time in our history when cultural restrictions and prohibitions have been reduced and the individual has taken center-stage. There are commodities in abundance for many, each with its own special magic. Anything seems possible. "The American Dream really should come true; certainly for me and perhaps even for everyone!" Our nation was long nourished by "rags-to-riches" Horatio Alger-type stories. "Perhaps the infantile desires for perfect peace, merger with mother but independence, too, and even happiness, can finally be realized!" Of course, we want action and excitement at times in order to avoid boredom, and we want merger with others on our terms. Omnipotence and omniscience should be available as a permanent fortress, unlike the ersatz version we manufacture from inside our magical bubbles where we live most of the time.

• • •

Meanwhile, the rich account for their fear and frustration by believing that if only they had more money, or better ways to flaunt it, they would finally achieve happiness. They continue the angry and greedy accumulation of wealth, "forgetting" the lessons of the past. Some of the poor have been convinced by cognitive capture that if only social interventions were lifted (big government) they would be happy. So government becomes the scapegoat and the poor support the reduction in taxes wanted by the rich. The poor will be even poorer as services are reduced. Big government becomes the stand-in for the bad parent who refused or was incapable of delivering on expectations and therefore needs to be punished. Anticipation of the defeat of the government as a stand-in for the father provides an exhilarating experience of power for both the rich and poor.[1] This is not to argue, however, that there is not plenty of room for improvement in the way our government functions, (Peter Orszag and John Bridgeland, *The Atlantic*, "Can Government Play Moneyball" July/August, 2013).

The critical need for everyone is to find some cure-all

that we can be angry about not having (this will motivate us) and to have some scapegoat we can blame for our fear. We need hope and an outlet for our anger. We start early, as already mentioned, to perceive our caregiver as magically omnipotent and omniscient. Just when we start to get hungry, they appear with our food so we feel they are part of us and we can magically control them. Older children often fear that their parents can read their minds. This creates a situation where it is easy to believe some leader can read our minds and could — and should — fix all of our problems. This is a pretty clear hold-over from infancy. The alternative of "tolerating the ambiguity," of perceiving life as basically tragic, as often incompatible with the reason we apply to it, has been described by Kurt Goldstein as "the only true heroism given to [our kind]."

But this largely unconscious fear and anger have provided the energy we needed in order to create the world we have: a world in which many, at least, can live better. That is, many have an abundance of material goods and a more comfortable, physical life. Competition, war and religion constitute the cultural frameworks we have created and preserved as containers and outlets for those feelings. Perhaps the wars were a necessary historical correlate to cultivating and harnessing that essential human energy, that energy and blood without which nothing happens.

• • •

We tend to think of the rows of quiet crosses in Arlington Cemetery when the results of wars are considered. The dead are no longer here to protest. Only the survivors of war live to tell about it and for them, perhaps it wasn't so bad. My friend Dan (to be described later) used his identity as a veteran to make him acceptable to himself and others. The wounded are still here haunting the hallways of the VA hospitals and some try to have an effect on us; we and the media show a remarkable facility for ignoring them. Should they complain too much, they then lose their claim to patriotism, which is a large part of their socially acceptable identity. If they complain too much, they may even lose the reason for their military sacrifice making life an empty, meaningless shell. It is as though war is a necessary catharsis and "force that gives us meaning." It has to happen periodically for society to be able to continue to function in its accustomed manner. Can we find a better way to make things work?

Again, "The mass of men lead lives of quiet desperation." Gum-chewers and smokers come to mind. Talking fast as though words were "sound-bites" or even bullets. Loud music with bright flashing lights. All these displace the quiet desperation — as does anger. Can we find better ways to express our anxiety and bring consciousness to bear on searching for better alternatives?

We seem to need some structure within which to focus our fear and anger. With the silence of despair, there are too many options, too much ambiguity; dark, mysterious fear floats to the surface of things. Competition, war and religion make up the structure we have created to facilitate and contain our fear and anger. Without that structure, we fear (again, mostly un-consciously) that our life forces might run in every conceivable direction, like the water behind a dam that has burst, or a river that has escaped its channels, or a picture that has escaped its frame, or a dancer that has leapt off the stage. Whether or not this kind of fear is justified is another question. Sometimes our fear is based on guilt and our felt need for punishment, sudden wealth syndrome being just one example. Experience indicates that our fear has unconscious origins and is out of proportion to the danger.

One explanation for this tendency is that we all sense, at some level of our being, that we are all at risk of going mad. We attempt to preserve the status quo: "Don't rock the boat or it might sink." And this fear is based on the truth: we are all subject to madness, given unbearable stress. The danger just gets magnified by our guilt and paranoia. Perhaps it is time now to explore our inner spaces and search for new structures of meaning and channels for our fear and energy that are less destructive to ourselves and our planet.

ENDNOTE

1   All power is unconsciously power over the father.

CHAPTER 7

Conscious and Unconscious Demons

The concept of demons has a long history in paganism, religion and Greek culture where Plato refers to the ideas of Socrates as demons. The term has been appropriated by psychology and is quite useful because it allows us to verbally designate human phenomena that we (as yet) do not fully comprehend. It conjures up the idea of vague but powerful forces that, like fear and love, are internal yet discrete. And, if they are discrete and at least labeled, we then have some hope of being able to identify them better in the future and so may be able eventually to control and modify them through personal effort.

We experience demons as forces, like fear, and then construct anti-demons to counter their influence. The anti-demons

77

we create are more available to consciousness. Usually we create anti-demons without being aware of the demon we are attempting to combat. Thus, people obsessed with power may deny any fear. The love demon may produce introversion in an attempt to gain protection. "If I do not leave the confines of my 'shell,' I won't have to feel the pain of others." The anti-demons can become negative demons that destroy our lives. Our fear may destroy us through our counter-measures.

The prototype for demons are the objects and forces we first encounter in infancy. This would be mother and the breast, father, siblings, caretakers, hunger, cold, sunlight, warmth — any objects and forces that make a lasting impression on our early consciousness. We come to understand vaguely that we are vulnerable to these things, but also that we have some control over them: crying elicits the breast, warmth, protection. We have the power of the smile to influence others and perhaps even demons. So begins the strategy of demons and counter-measures. Later, it seems to dawn on us that if we can control them, we can also invent our own demons to gain the comforting belief that we do have control over our lives. But this is mostly an unconscious process, so as adults we must first become conscious of the demons before we can understand our anti-demons.

Later in life, or whenever we encounter the enigma of death, we may objectify the missing person by considering him/her as a kind of demon, or hallucinate sightings of the person:

hear their voice, see them in dreams.

For this discussion, I find 'demon' and 'anti-demon' the most useful words in our language to utilize for an exploration of unconscious processes wherein powerful forces act on our lives in ways (good or bad) that we do not fully understand. It is an attempt to grapple with mysterious and "slippery forces."

• • •

Our number one demon is *fear of insignificance*: the "chilling thought" of being forgotten which includes, by implication, death. It is so powerful that we cannot fully acknowledge it. In literature, we acknowledge this conflict between our feeling of importance versus our knowledge and fear of insignificance as riddles. The most famous perhaps being the ancient Greek riddle of the Sphinx in "Oedipus Rex" by Sophocles.

The story is that the Sphinx is eating the young men of the town of Thebes who cannot answer her riddle.[1] The town offers that anyone who can deliver the town from this demon will become King and can marry the widowed Queen. This riddle embodies human insignificance as it is about human movement from childhood to old age and death. It is hard to solve because we deny our death and the process of aging. We exclude that process from our consciousness in an attempt to avoid the pain of that awareness. But the death-demon never goes away.

Death-denial is one of our anti-demons and gets us in a lot of trouble. It makes realistic plans for the future more problematic.

The riddle: What walks on four legs in the morning, two legs in the afternoon and three legs at night? The answer is simple: man. For we start life crawling on all fours, then walk on two legs as adults and finally use a cane when we grow old. Oedipus solves the riddle in two ways: first, he gives the right answer to the Sphinx and second, he gets to marry the Queen who, unbeknownst to him, is his mother. This is his reward for slaying the man-devouring Sphinx (she jumps off a cliff after Oedipus answers the riddle), which equates with symbolic immortality by way of fucking mother so you can be reborn. Sound crazy? Our unconscious is capable of a lot more crazy things than that. It/we are desperate for solutions to the "riddle of life" and our significance within that riddle. Fantasies do give us some temporary satisfaction. This, at least, explains the madness of the anti-demon incest that takes place now.

The anti-demon incest is a good example of how our anti-demons get us in trouble. They hold out promises they cannot keep. Racism and extermination don't work either: the insignificance demon never goes away; it follows us to the grave irregardless (sic). But the promises of immortality through incest are no less preposterous than the anti-demon idea that there is some after-life, where we will be rewarded for our good works on earth or punished for our evil. It is more acceptable because it has more adherents, more "accomplices." Our rewards more likely come in this life by a feeling of peace and wisdom when we know we have done the right thing. But we are so desperate to solve the "riddle" that when our unconscious proposes an anti-demon to solve the riddle, we devour it hook, line and sinker. It needs to be "said" however, that many of the ideas proposed by the unconscious are plausible. It is the assigned task of the ego to determine whether or not the ideas from the unconscious are plausible. Most of the ideas in this book came from my unconscious. You may disagree with my finding of plausibility, but it is the plausible ideas throughout history that have resulted in progress.

There is a similar riddle in Puccini's opera *Turandot*, which is based on poetry by a 12th century Persian. Princess Turandot, like the Sphinx, is causing death by killing any suitors that cannot answer her three riddles. Prince Calàf answers the three riddles but then Turandot (who seems to hate all men) tries to renege on the deal: "Will you take me by force?" So Prince Calàf makes her a proposition: "If you can tell me my name before sunrise you may kill me." The "femme fatale" is a symbol for both the cold-hearted mother who denies us sex and rebirth and hence, immortality, and also the inevitability of death. But also significant here is that she doesn't know his name; hence, she can imagine him as anyone she wants, including her father. With this incentive, she falls in love with the Prince; they marry and presumably "live happily ever after." The audience gets the vicarious satisfaction of seeing and feeling the protagonist conquer both death and the reluctant mother. For it seemed at the outset that his death was inevitable; that he would be beheaded like all the other unsuccessful suitors for Turandot. So the riddles and demons about life, love and death have been around for a long time, and it seems we can only solve them in fantasy.

Symbolically, the riddles about death reflect not only our fear of death but also, how to solve the riddle that death not only comes inevitably, but it haunts us for all of our lives. Thus, it is the fear of death that is more of a problem than death itself. The answer implied by the riddles is that the truly brave can answer the riddle because they are not afraid of death; they are true heroes. The answer for all of us is that if we can turn away from our essentially futile and violent pursuits of immortality, in religious or sectarian forms, then we can invest our energies more in the satisfactions of the present. The capacity of parents to transmit this life-orientation to their children is embodied in the previously cited expression: "If the parents have the courage to die, the children will have the courage to live."

Both Oedipus and Calàf impress us as doing something realistic; they are putting an end to death. But it is realistic because we know that, at least theoretically, we *can* put an end to the fear of death, and *that* is the real demon in our lives. Partly, it is a demon because it reflects our insignificance: "How could I possibly be as significant as I feel I am, if I'm just going to die?"

As an aside about *Turandot*, Puccini was unable to finish this opera before he died. He lived long enough but couldn't do it. My theory is he couldn't make the music work because the storyline is so unrealistic, and Puccini was a realist. Most of his operas end in tragedy. The idea of a cold, vicious woman suddenly being converted into a warm, loving, ideal mother-type was just too far-fetched for him to be able to set that conversion to music.

We build many anti–demons without being aware of the demon(s) that precipitates the anti or defensive demon.[2] This demon is powerful because it is true. Hence, the real enemy is reality. That is, in the grand scheme of things, we are all insignificant. When we are all annihilated by whichever terminal disaster comes along, there will be no one left to remember any of us; we will all be exquisitely forgotten: blank oblivion will reign supreme. This fear-demon is so painful for our sense of who we are that it remains buried in layers of the unconscious.

The effects of this fear permeate our culture. It starts early with sibling rivalry, where each sibling acts more or less like a chick in the nest who knows there is not enough food for all the chicks; only the most aggressive will survive. Later in life, the pattern continues as hazing rituals in schools, initiation ceremonies in clubs and fraternities and competition in business and sports. It seems that bread is not the "staff-of-life"— recognition is. But we deny this and pretend to be civilized and decent and make scapegoats of savages that hunt heads. Small wonder so many adolescents experience despair. There is even a game teen-aged boys play where they stand around drinking beer until someone falls down drunk; then the rest piss on him, thus reflecting the values of their culture.

We invent many kinds of anti-demons to rescue us from the fear of insignificance, of not being fed, but the rescue may turn into a capture as we frantically invest more and more energy in our anti-demons. For the delusion of a rescue is always tenuous at best, and needs to be "shored up" by greater and greater commitments and sacrifices of self and/or others. Thus the anti-demon invented for our rescue becomes our tormentor. The demons dwell in the unconscious, and from there, pull the controlling strings of our marionette-like lives.

Two glaring examples of the destructive anti-demons we create in order to combat this fear are racism and anti-Semitism. Martin Luther King, Jr. refers to "nobodyness" in a letter from jail to white ministers: blacks "are forever fighting a degenerating sense of "nobodyness."[3] Racism provides more than just a scapegoat; it provides "proof" that the feared insignificance of the persecutors has not only been identified and made manifest, but has been found to reside in a particular segment of society. Thus, it has been effectively disowned and eliminated from the fears of the dominant population!

One of the results of the Civil War was to threaten the defeated southern society with "nobodyiness." Intuitively, leaders quickly set to work to transfer those agonizing fears and feelings of "nobodyiness" on to the most vulnerable portion of the society, and to even punish them for being such "nobodies." Desperate to purge the society of such "chilling thoughts," they ridiculed and murdered to protect themselves from insignificance. To use Leo Bersani's term (*Intimacies*, p. 55), they expanded their egos at the expense of the egos of the black subculture. Such "cultural gymnastics," however, are never entirely convincing to white people — especially for those who experienced more love and devotion from their black nursemaids than from their own white mothers, and may have played baseball and gone fishing with, and even loved, their black playmates. But this sense of a contradiction and/or guilt simply requires an increase in the racism anti-demon in order to counteract any doubts. The fear of the "nobodyness" demon never goes away and must be frequently addressed by invoking the violence, physical and psychological, of the racist anti-demon. The "expanded ego" shrinks over time.

Our current plague of the celebrityitis anti-demon is basically an attempt to gain significance, to expand our egos, to hold at bay our fears of the "nobodyness" demon.

There are similar dynamics involved in German anti-Semitism. Germany was also a defeated nation after World War I. It must have galled the defeated Germans, already threatened with "nobodyness," to have in their midst a people alleging to have the significance of being God's chosen people. "We will decide who is 'nobody' in this society; we will prove it is the Jews, and by exterminating them, we will eliminate all traces of 'nobodyness' in our land!"

Ironically, it is we who create our anti-demons and then we fall victim to our own attempts at self-rescue.

• • •

Another unconscious demon we have to contend with might be called a *hope-demon*. It is the hope that we can regress to infancy where we felt safer; or rather, we attempt to resurrect that time and part of our infancy where we felt safe. The unconscious is an accomplished artist in this regard; it can reconstruct the past selectively in ways that provide consolation. This is a necessary therapy for the human condition — to be able to retreat to a safe place periodically in order to escape from current trials and tribulations, to "recreate" the self. We only get in trouble with this hope-demon when we take ourselves too seriously and demand that all current experiences conform to those infantile hopes and expectations. Thus the demon we must confront is that, while temporary "visits" to infancy serve to restore some hope and vigor, we must not expect our adult lives to comply with infantile expectations. The widespread use of alcohol testifies to the need for a kind of escapism. The advantage of alcohol is that the next morning, the escape has escaped; we are once again struggling with reality. The hope-demon stays in the unconscious; no one will admit, and probably is not even aware, of the infantile origins of their behavior.

We see this demon in control in people who demand

to be the center of attention as though they were the only important person in the room. Oddly enough, this kind of infantile behavior is frequently found in leaders who, once they take on this demon as their guide to glory, struggle desperately and sometimes successfully to prove it is true. Others in the society, less infantile but still yearning for powerful parental figures as guides, may appreciate the arrogance of the infantile behavior, and be comforted by the feeling that the leader can protect them and make sense out of life. But again, the infantile demon is unconscious. Those responding to this demon simply feel entitled to special, privileged treatment without realizing the connection to infancy.

• • •

Third on the list is the demon of *ambiguity*. This demon has grown more prevalent in recent times as societies fragment and the world becomes smaller. We used to live, for the most part, in stable communities where world-views were consistent. In our times, the media and cheap, convenient travel to other lands expose us to multiple world-views different from our own. Even within small communities, there are usually sources of conflict over how the world and our individual lives should be perceived and conducted. None of this is bad; it can even be stimulating. But for those who cannot tolerate the ambiguity, frustration may lead to attempts to impose consensus and the search for scapegoats to blame and punish for the perceived painful ambiguity. So again, by identifying this demon, this tendency toward unwarranted violence, we can keep watch over and perhaps even domesticate this demon. To the extent that a period of ambiguity can help us to solve problems, it is a friendly demon. It is only when our fear of ambiguity instigates anti-ambiguity demons that we get in trouble.

Related to ambiguity, but not exactly its opposite is our fear of chaos and creation of meaning as an anti-demon. We feel we must and can understand everything that goes on. These people are victims of the anti-chaos demon. Science and technology have encouraged us in this quest and some of us have "latched on" to meaning as the panacea for all ills. They go so far as to create magical explanations when science fails or when science delivers explanations that make them uncomfortable. Fetishes of one kind or another top the list of anti-chaos demons. Our culture provides any number of fetishized commodities: fancy cars, clothes, homes and vacations will establish the meaning we require (and our significance). Any number of religious zealots will provide a clearly articulated world-view wherein we are important and protected by magical/supernatural powers. Culture can tolerate a certain amount of this without sacrificing efficacy in problem solving. It is only when these "meaning-freaks" gain power in the decision-making processes (as they have today) that we are faced with a dangerous anti-demon. Such conviction in an anti-chaos demon of one kind or another resides not just in elected officials, but in the many meaning-creating institutions such as the media, entertainment and sports institutions all of which influence public opinion.

Those "possessed by this anti-chaos meaning anti-demon" are convinced that they are the only ones who know the truth; they are, or have access to, those magical beings who are omniscient. This demon resides in the unconscious where it "feeds on" infantile memories of omniscient and omnipotent parents. We need some way to exorcise these demons before their "truth" leads to the premature failure of the "human experiment." We need to improve our ability to "tolerate the ambiguity" of chaos and not knowing.

• • •

Fourth in this "short list" of demons is *power*. Our demonic ideas of power, like meaning, have origins in infantile fantasies of parents, but include the conviction that although the most powerful parent (gender is not so important) was omnipotent, he or she still constitutes a reasonable pathway to our own power. The cliché is that all power is power over the father. We experience that parent's power as transferable to us if we can "play our cards right." The most straight-forward strategy is the son killing the father as in the Oedipal Complex, and gaining the title and power of king and the mother. But we have invented myriad ways to magically reinvent or steal our parents so we can steal their power and punish them for not being perfect. Marriage counselors must contend with these dynamics on a daily basis as spouses complain about partners who didn't live up to "expectations."

This demon causes us trouble because we are convinced that omnipotence is available in some way when, in fact, it is not. No matter how competitive we are, how much money and how many armies we acquire, we still cannot have the absolute power we imagine. We can, for instance, control the bodies of others but not their hearts and minds. Nor can we avoid random tragedies or our own death. But many still pursue power as though it will solve all of their problems, wrecking havoc on many lives, including their own because of this demon.

The anti-power demon is the abandonment of the pursuit of any and all power. By refusing to participate in the frenzied competition for power, we control this unconscious demon but sacrifice many opportunities for self-fulfillment in the process.

• • •

The fifth demon here is the most difficult. It is *sex*. Sex never takes place without the presence of myriad unconscious demons. It is doubtful if it would be any fun without them. So it is not a matter of eliminating demons from our sex lives, but rather excluding some of the more radical ones and making the remaining ones follow our rules for the game. Adam Phillips (on page 41 of "Desiring by Myself," which is Chapter 4 of *Longing*, edited by Jean Petrucelli, 2006) puts it succinctly: "Our wishes are unmarried to the world."

Being a heterosexual male, I am most familiar with the shadowy figures which enter into that sexual arrangement. All these demons have fun with our sexual activity. Reentering the vagina is in part a return to the womb where it is safe and, at our leisure, we can be born over again to live a better life and avoid death. Thus we, and some of our demons, enjoy ecstasy and power as we feel a sense of living out that fantasy. This gives us power and access to infantile fantasies, which are also attached to that era. We feel we will be the only one doing this, so we will be significant and understand things better than anyone else and thus have more power and meaning. In my kind of sex, we are certainly stealing mother away from father, and this may engender guilt and fear of punishment. Women, in turn, are stealing father away from mother. This is one reason so many prefer sex in a dark room. We are "getting away with something."

The guilt sometimes surrounding sex — because of these complicated dynamics and the rage when we realize or suspect that it is only a fantasy — leads some to change partners frequently in a frantic search for the one who will make all the fantasies come true. They are so busy chasing demons, they never have the opportunity to get to know their partners and experience intimacy. This is a minor problem compared to those who become so obsessed that the sex-demons completely control their lives in the form of child pornography, or molesting children, or sadomasochistic tragedies or incest. Again, we will never eliminate these demons, but if we can understand them better in the next 200 years perhaps we can diminish their sometimes destructive influence.

One reason for the frequent change of partners and even anonymous sex is that we can more readily let our imagination run wild with a partner we don't know. This is why prostitutes and even blow-up dolls work so well; our imagination has free rein. Once you know your partner, your imagination is confined to more realistic limits. But this reining-in of sexual imagination produces a stabilizing effect on society.

• • •

The last and most pathetic of our demons to be considered here is the *victim demon*. When this demon is in charge, or to the extent it is present, we are convinced that our suffering will call forth a magical rescue. This is related to masochism, but in pure masochism the goal has been reduced to the suffering itself; pain is the end goal. The victim-demon has roots in early experiences in which suffering did actually result in a sense of rescue of one kind or another. In the unconscious, it happened "yesterday," and for those in thrall to this demon, they feel it could quite logically happen again whenever it is needed. Thus the relationship to distress becomes one of a comforting expectation of rescue: "Where is my rescuer? Where is it? I know it's here somewhere." And again, like Charlie Brown with the football, we never learn from our disappointments. The expectation of rescue remains rock-solid in the unconscious. Not, it is true, as a suitable plan for the future, but more as an echo from a benevolent past — enough to interfere with the most practicable plans and actions.

All of these demons operate in the unconscious so as to distort our perception of what we can reasonably expect to achieve in life. Recognizing their influence helps us to understand what we can actually expect in the future from reality. We will probably achieve less power with this understanding, but we will be less driven and frustrated and will have more time for intimate connections with others. More important, it will become easier for us to cooperate in solving the urgent problems that threaten the survival of our species and our planet. It will help us to make peace instead of war.

ENDNOTES

1   Since women are the givers of life it is quite natural to presume they take it away also: The extremes touch.

2   "Reaction formation" is the appropriate term in psychology.

3   See *The Civil Rights Act's Unsung Victory* by Randall Kennedy in the June 2014 *Harper's* (p. 37).

CHAPTER 8

Second Order Demons

This second order of demons is more easily witnessed; not so deeply buried in the unconscious, but just as pernicious in their effects on our lives.

For openers, it is as though the whole country — and much of the world — is caught up in a *euphoric expectation of some ill-defined success or happiness,* and at the same time is terrified of failure and punishment. We are terrified of the tragedies, ambiguity and chaos, and invent myriad defenses. Among the defenses is the "great expectation" of good things to come. These defenses and demons make any kind of understanding of why we're doing what we're doing extremely difficult. In addition, all social identity, like fame, is nebulous and temporary and when we do gain some measure of importance, we fear losing it altogether, becoming socially invisible. If we can "catch" it, we can also lose it. Significance is always nebulous and ultimately bound for blank oblivion because it can only truly exist in the hearts and minds of other people, irregardless [sic] of the tombstones, monuments and history books. At some level of consciousness we know this and tremble: more fear and frustration.

The fact that most of these processes are unconscious makes our current social turmoil more difficult to understand and address. We're not able to see the core of the problem; hence, my recommendation for 200 years of exploring "inner space." For instance, a better acquaintance with some of our unconscious fears would lessen our obsession with guns and warfare. Painful disillusionment is endemic to growing up (again, Rodin's "Prodigal Son" or "Despairing Adolescent"), but we seem to ignore it and still expect our children to be happy and even to please their parents. Sometimes we insist, in subtle and unconscious ways, that they be happy so we can forget our own sorrows; the children can act as antidepressants for the parents. This often leads to an adult attitude of: "Life is not fair; no one cares about me; someone has to pay; let's go to war or stab children on the elevator," (which recently happened in Brooklyn, N.Y.)

The rich pretend to be satisfied so they will appear successful and the rest of us will be envious. But they play a valuable role in our lives. Societies always invent and support some kind of magical entities — gods, royalty, nobility, upper classes, celebrities — so they can feel that there are some who escape the frustration-trap.[1] We need to at least have that vicarious satisfaction, and/or even better, see a possibility for our own "success." We need to keep the idea and hope of happiness alive in the hearts and minds of people. But there is no human behavior that does not begin with frustration and involve uncertain results regardless of how much you own or know.

We would do well to listen to some of our "in-house" prophets like Keynes, who predicted in 1932 that the love of money would one day "be recognized [as]... one of those... semi-pathological propensities which one hands over with a shudder to the specialists in mental disease." Also germane here is Thorstein Veblen's concept of "conspicuous consumption" (homes with 10 bedrooms? or 10 homes?), which we understand now serve mainly to create envy in others. Adam Phillips: "One response to frustration is to invent something to be tempted by," (like money or some version of a Moby Dick); "Greed is despair about pleasure," (*Missing Out*, p. xix)

We have grown and prospered with this new American culture for over 200 years. Contemplating this initial stretch of our history, I attempt to grasp four of our second order demons by a meaningful part of their "anatomy." The decline in religiosity is perhaps the most salient, and three other trends seem to have been waiting in the wings to take up the resulting "cultural slack." To a large extent, religion has been replaced by the idea of celebrity status, spectacle and celebration: celebrityitis.

We used to go to the circus once a year to be over-entertained by the three-ring circus. Now we have a 12- or even 120-ring circus to watch in our homes every night. We have become so proficient at imitating celebrities that many people seem to go through life as though they were acting in a continuous movie in which they are the star. This shades off now into worship of celebrities, other idols and self, instead of a God and/or love.

• • •

The second trend, or new demon, is our burgeoning and naïve *faith in scientific and economic progress*, such that the talents of people and resources of the earth can be combined and developed in an infinite spiral of increasing individual and social gratification. You may have to read between the lines to recognize this but it seems to underlie many of our policy decisions and indecisions. Only something akin to faith in magic can sustain such a utopian belief — or another beneficent but "invisible hand." But the popularity of the prosperity gospel, of gambling casinos and the absence of floor '13's all testify to our continuing belief in magic. We praise science but ignore it when it contradicts our magical beliefs. At bottom, it reveals our conviction that the earth is separate from us; it is there to be exploited by us instead of an integral part of our history, our existence and our destiny.

• • •

A third demon and trend was born during this interval — a new value, a new form of heroism connected to the other trends. And a new phrase was coined: *"getting away with it"* (Phillips, *Missing Out*, p. 98). This slang expression originated in the U.S. — it is as American as apple pie. It seems to be intertwined with our declining religiosity and increasing faith in entrepreneurial and scientific success.

This trend perhaps grew out of the heroic tradition of classical Greek culture. Our increasing emphasis on the individual as separate from community has seen ups and downs, but in the intervening 2,000 years has gradually increased to where many refuse to be submerged in community; the celebrity stands out from, and above, community. It is the individual, for the most part, who "gets away with it." Corporations and even nations can sometimes "get away with it" but a whistle-blower is a constant danger and "thorn-in-the-side." Settlers to a new land are more apt to be individualistic than those who stay behind in the home country, and prosperity nurtures that self-sufficient attitude. Celebrities are notoriously individualistic.

The trend, or demon, identified as "getting away with it," deserves a closer look. It may have started with a few insiders treating the rules as something to be broken with impunity. And/or it could have been a simple outgrowth of our "getting away with" building a new and thriving society on land we pretty much stole from native Indians, Mexicans, Hawaiians (we stole it fair and square), Spanish and native Alaskans. The "good life" as something where ethical behavior, character, responsibilities toward others and love were important, no longer enters the picture. Those things are either on the "back-burner" or not on the stove at all. Material qualities are the only recognized criterion for respect. There have always been some deviants getting away with things: an extreme example being the sociopaths. But when a new value-loaded phrase is coined and is in common usage in a language, it indicates a change in the values of a whole population. The new definition of success became accumulating wealth and/or fame and not getting caught, regardless of how you do it — including "getting away with murder." Or "Lance Armstrong, all American boy" and Governor Chris Christie almost "got away with it," and we're not surprised.

But as this new basic value, this new form of heroism, permeated society and spread, it weakened the respect for others and the rules that used to hold society together. It seems that an increasingly large part of our society treats the rules as only straw dogs: something to destroy or evade in order to exploit the system, to make a profit and not get caught (hedge fund managers and mortgage brokers in Chicago come to mind).[2] Meanwhile, the rest of society is punished for any trespass against the rules, and expected to maintain order and continue to respect and obey the law. The contradiction in expectations becomes more and more apparent. About seven million adults in the U.S.

are under some type of adult correctional supervision at this time (2.9%). One and a half million of these are in prison. A society exposed to the "getting away with it" kind of disparity will soon show signs of disintegration: bizarre behavior, increasing conflict, and use of force and surveillance by society to achieve containment and punishment. Sound familiar? It seems we are there. It is more efficient to control a society with religion than with police and the courts, but this seems no longer to be an option in the U.S. Been there, done that!

Looking at this situation more from the unconscious perspective, it seems we have arrived at a place in our socio-cultural evolution where many of the rich want to conserve a system equivalent to a surrogate god — the laws of the land — for the emotional comfort a quasi-god provides. At the same time, however, they attack or at least subvert the power of the "father" by hiring accountants and attorneys who are professional loophole finders, thereby increasing their wealth and fantasy of power over the God/father. All power is experienced unconsciously as power over the father. In this unconscious power nexus, again, pleasure always fails and "failed pleasure becomes greed."

ENDNOTES

1   There is another side to "inventing celebrities" for public

consumption. The public also knows it can destroy the famous; vent its anger on those who fail to live up to expectations. There is a long tradition of this; James Frazier in *The Golden Baugh* describes some of the roots. If tragedy struck an ancient society, they might kill the king for not doing his job well enough. The famous also seem to be aware of this and sometimes tremble, for the public does have a large say in who deserves to be famous and whether their fame "lives or dies." Mayan kings would mutilate their genitals to appease the gods. Again, we are inescapably social animals.

2   See facts on mortgage brokers in *The Case for Reparations* by Ta-Nehisi Coates in June 2014 *The Atlantic.*

CHAPTER 9

Is War Avoidable?

How many battleships could we fill with the blood shed from our 3,023 wars? We attempt to ignore this evidence of our vicious nature, but for most of us it will not go away, no matter how hard we try. The dead were our relatives and their deaths — and all of the homeless and hungry in the world — loom on the horizon of our consciousness like dark threatening storm clouds of guilt. We sometimes even kill others and ourselves in the attempt to expunge and/or cover over our guilt and anger.

This excludes, however, those already in the Hell of not being able to love in the first place. If you're not connected to others by affection, you may feel very little guilt and may even feel joy when others suffer or when you yourself do violence to others. "Misery loves company." Perhaps these are the ones who perpetrate wars; perhaps they are desperate for some kind of connection with others and violence is the only pathway they have experienced. Or perhaps we are all capable of vicious behavior given the right circumstances. I suppose we would not have survived as a species otherwise. Leaders already in the "no-love Hell" know how to play on the feelings of their followers to bring out their vicious nature. And we are only too happy to oblige: "War is a force that gives us meaning."

Returning to the War of 1812, a single U.S. soldier had a significant impact on that war by killing General Robert Ross as he led the British army toward Baltimore. The soldier was a sniper, or sharpshooter, and probably knew that if he fired on the enemy, he would be discovered and killed. He fired. He killed the General. The General's escort killed him.[1] Americans retreated and the British continued their advance on Baltimore defeating another defensive stand of Americans within five miles of Baltimore. It's unclear why the British then stopped and retreated; perhaps because British ships were unable to proceed up the Patapsco River and provide naval support for the ground invasion. The Americans had anticipated this strategy, and had blocked the channel to Baltimore by sinking some of their ships in the Patapsco River. The death of Ross was probably also significant as well as the failure to capture Fort McHenry.

Part of the invading British were mercenary soldiers; not British citizens and some were American slaves who had escaped to the British and been trained and armed by them and served as guides, pilots and infantry.[2] Key makes reference to this in the third stanza of his poem: "No refuge could save the hireling and slave." This was a sensitive stanza in later years when we were on good terms with England because it "cast aspersions on the British." This stanza, which begins: "And where are the foes who so vauntingly swore," is usually omitted today from copies and performances of the song. General Ross reportedly swore he would spend the winter of 1814-15 in Baltimore and said: "I don't care if it rains militia."

• • •

Is there a way we can "call the hands" of leaders when they begin to play on our conscious and unconscious propensities for violence? Can we examine our expectations for pleasure, punishment and competition and adjust them more toward mutual cooperation? This would lessen the chances of future wars. Can we uncover and enhance the beautiful part of the human spirit? Can we help others to feel love? The very life of our planet is on the bargaining table. Is it possible to find consolation in our connections with other members of the human race who are all similarly burdened? "Thanks Mom" by Scott Stossel (*The Atlantic*, May 2013) reports that "Happiness is love," backed by 75 years of Harvard research.[3] If we cannot get that message, which has been around for a long time, perhaps "… the human experiment will [fail]" (Deepak Chopra, "The Big Question," *The Atlantic*, July/August 2013). How can we recognize the delusional nature of our expectations of happiness through acquiring "things" and manipulating and competing with others, and realize that we get more from giving than we get from getting? How can we achieve healthy functioning in spite of whatever dose of anxiety we have to deal with, as cited earlier in Stossel's other *The Atlantic* article, "Surviving Anxiety."

Adam Phillips helps us to understand the gravity of the situation: "Being a person is virtually or potentially intolerable unless you are lucky enough to live in a time of war," (*Promises, Promises*, p. 46). It seems the difficulty of being human demands conflict and violence of one kind or another. Perhaps we can only know who we are when we collide with one another. In addition, the terror and anxiety of war enable us to locate a source for our own free-floating terror and anxiety. Conor McCarthy makes such a connection for Joseph Conrad: "The War [WW I] has allowed Conrad's psyche to purge itself of terror and anxiety.[4]" The problem then may not be to eliminate conflict, but to regulate it in such a way as to minimize the damage to one another and the planet. This is why sports are so important. Seen in that light, perhaps the brain concussions of football players are a necessary evil. Or perhaps the way our societies emphasize the self over connections with others needs to be reconsidered, as Leo Bersani and Adam Phillips suggest in "Intimacies."

There will be no love without an openness to others. Others are a part of reality. Hence, if we are preoccupied with shutting out reality in order to protect our treasured sense of an inflated ego, we will not be able to let others in and experience love — whatever love is. This is why I believe it is so important we recognize reality as much as we can, with its ambiguities, terrors and disappointments. That is the price we must pay for love, which is the one thing that will make life worthwhile.

• • •

Francis Scott Key lived to be 63 having witnessed and taken significant parts in the formation of our country. He died of pneumonia in 1843 while visiting his daughter, Elizabeth, in Baltimore. He became familiar with death at an early age: when he was three his baby sister died at the age of eight months. Another baby sister was born when he was four; she survived and became his adored and adoring playmate. Infant deaths were more common then and his parent's record of four births and two survivals was close to the norm. I suggest that — because death was more frequent — it was harder to deny at that time in our history, and therefore we were closer to death, nature and reality. Death is a large part of nature and reality and when we deny death, as we do today, we block out; we cut ourselves off from much of the natural world and the people, plants and animals that live here with us.

There is a pattern in Key's life worth exploring. He was deeply religious; according to Delaplaine (*Francis Scott Key*), "When any unfavorable events came to pass, he cringed in terror because of what he regarded as a manifestation of Divine disapproval. ... God was not a benevolent spirit, but an irascible Sovereign ... whose chief duty was to reward and chastise. ... all things are ordered according to a divine plan." In addition, Key was warmly attached to his mother in a way that suggests he owed her some great debt. Again from Delaplaine in a letter from Key to his mother in 1807, when Key was 28: "I would rather see you satisfied and hear you say with joy 'this is my son' than receive the applause of the whole world." Key was obviously a sensitive soul, a poet and a peacemaker. When his baby sister died at the age of eight months, Key was three and at that age when sibling rivalry and competition are often present. If he experienced some animosity toward this usurper of his only-child status — and then the child died — it might have left deep wounds of guilt, especially on such a sensitive and caring personality.

A child of three may retain some feelings of magical omnipotence; he might have been tortured by guilt that he couldn't or wouldn't save the baby, as well as guilt that he wanted her gone and may have caused her death. Deep feelings of religiosity, including the belief that all things are arranged by God (which means, at least partly, I didn't do it), would be one possible reaction to this trauma, one defense against guilt. However, guilt comes in the "back door," with the conviction that God is punishing you for something you have done when things go wrong. In addition, feelings of betrayal of the loving and now distraught mother for the same constellation of feelings, and guilt toward her could be a part of this pattern. Obviously this is conjecture, but it probes the human condition and our unconscious demons. One thing that is not conjecture is that whatever the combination of genetic and experiential factors in Key's life, they produced a sensitive and creative artist who gave us a national treasure and a life worthy of study, if not emulation.

Key lived to see the deaths of three of his sons: Edward drowned in 1822 in the Potomac River at age eight; Daniel challenged another man to a dual and was killed in 1836 at age 20; John Ross died of a sudden disease in 1837 at age 29, leaving a wife and two small children. Another tragedy for Key was the sudden death of a young woman in Alabama. She was the wife of the governor whom he had met and grown fond of while on that peace-making mission for President Jackson. They corresponded and wrote poetry about one another; the relationship was platonic. They met in 1833; she died of lockjaw (apparently tetanus) in 1835 at age 31.

Key's life was characterized more by despair than by fear and anger, perhaps a prerequisite for a peacemaker. After Key's death, the family tradition of tragedy and despair was carried on by his son, Philip Barton Key, who, as previously mentioned, was shot and killed in 1859 (age 40) by an irate husband, when it was revealed that his wife was having an affair with Philip. In 1962, another descendent of Key, William Ward Clore, Jr. (a first cousin and friend of mine) challenged, and was taken hostage by, bank robbers in Tuscon, Arizona. He was the bank teller asked by the bank manager to bring the $10,000 that the robbers stole. His whereabouts were unknown for five years until his remains were accidentally located in the Arizona desert. He was 31 when he was killed and also left two small children. We are all vulnerable.

So, once again, why 3,023 wars? My answer: Because we cannot accept the difficulty of life: our fear and anger, our insignificance, weakness, chaos and ignorance. We have constantly to "prove" we are in control of our lives, brave, strong and smart, and much more so than others. We are born afraid, weak, ignorant and angry and spend the rest of our lives trying to prove that this is not so, to escape from that terror. From the beginning, we sense that without a competent caregiver, we will die, and that our caregivers do not always love us.[5] It is terrifying to be a weak and vulnerable being in the midst of mysterious, innumerable and unspeakable dangers. "Mom and Dad must be omniscient and omnipotent and love me very much so I can feel safe." But very soon we find that this is not the case and begin to hate them for letting us down, and to fear them because we hate them. Lower class children find out sooner than children from other classes because their protection is less secure. Children of all classes have been known to leave home in search of their "real parents," i.e., the ones they imagined they had when they were infants and felt safe. War and humiliation of others in general (making others envious), give us the satisfaction of the pursuit, if not the possession, of ultimate power and knowledge so we can feel safe again.

These are our basic unconscious demons resulting from our infantile vulnerability and fear. It is remembered (in the unconscious, it happened yesterday), carried over to the present and expected in the future. Because our identity is socially determined, we are always at the mercy of public opinion. As a single individual, we are physically and psychologically helpless against the many. Because human existence is basically a mystery, we can never achieve complete understanding; we are ignorant. And yet, we feel that we cannot let ourselves experience the despair that this produces, which is the only way to improve our situation.

Another popular escape from despair is the cult figure and magic in general, a place where we can submit to cognitive capture by others in return for magical reassurances. Some preachers will even promise God-given success if we pay them money. Even Freud and subsequent self-fashioned psychoanalytic heroes need to be shelved so we can practice the more difficult art of informality (Adam Phillips, *Promises, Promises*, p. 111), so we can get to know one another and ourselves better.

• • •

Caveat:

In the unlikely event that some substantial portion[6] of

society breaks out of the stifling uniformity of the well-structured self, the results are impossible to predict at this time. The virtual self is unlimited. It has yet to be charted. Violence would decrease; I believe we can expect that much, for the well-structured and therefore predictable self is — at its deepest levels — frustrated, angry and prone to a soul-satisfying violence. But currently, we seem to feel we must maintain the assigned self-façade to the very bottom of the grave. The idea of an experience of self-shattering of the self (Bersani and Phillips, *Intimacies*, p. 92) is anathema to us and yet this is the one pathway open to us for the full experience of the human potential and love for self, others and the earth.

As a "watered-down" version of such a profound shift in self-perception, we might at least rearrange our priorities to something where material things, money and power are not the most important aspects of life. But even that would produce drastic and unanticipated social and economic consequences. If, for instance, the rich were to recognize that their sense of superiority was based on the fact that others envy them and that they are not really happy, large segments of society would no longer be so frustrated and angry about not having the money that was felt to be the "answer" to happiness.

They would have a new demon to wrestle with: that the happiness promised by our culture, doesn't exist. Then they wouldn't work as hard for that goal of happiness. Fewer workers at Google, for instance, would be willing to give the 110%

effort expected there and at so many other corporations. The world might become more like Greece, where perhaps the very old happiness myth has worn out. We are unable at this time to predict the nature of those consequences. I can only hope that future savants will have achieved a more adequate understanding of human nature and social dynamics when and if that event takes place.

As it is, we spend most of our lives in the pursuit of delusions of happiness and/or victory in the midst of psychological and physical violence, sometimes killing ourselves and/or others accidentally or deliberately in the process. However, this energy turns the wheels of our economy. Without it I can only guess at the consequences. Perhaps we would abandon competition and achieve a comfortable level of living for everyone, and enjoy the camaraderie, love, sex and adventure available to us. Perhaps we would learn to celebrate the mystery instead of being dominated, tormented, frustrated and terrorized by it. Or, at the other extreme, perhaps depression would so change life-goals that people would not show up for work and chaos would prevail. Many other societies, or human experiments, throughout history have failed.

Much as we would like to believe it, our environment, physical and social, is not static, but is rather in constant flux. Our fate is inextricably bound up with those environments, and we will live or die, prosper or perish, depending on those vagaries — fantasies of space voyages and religious/magical/parental rescues notwithstanding.

There is a parallel in the way many people treat their bodies. There is a presumption or fantasy of stability and persistence of both physical and social environments that supports smoking, obesity, drinking and drugs to excess, inadequate exercise and reckless exploitation of the environment. To recognize the transient nature of our bodies and our connection to death and the earth increases anxiety, but encourages a healthier lifestyle and stewardship of the earth. Some degree of acceptance of death makes life more precious. This is more difficult for the lower classes, because they are already plagued with fears of social death and find that eating, smoking, drinking and polluting reduce anxiety temporarily. We can and must apply ourselves as diligently as possible to taking care of our bodies and our earth so our species may survive as long as possible — so that love may endure.

ENDNOTES

1   There are three candidates for the killer of Ross. American sources identify two men: Daniel Wells and Henry G. McComas both of whom fired at the General and both were killed in the following action. British accounts name one Aquila Randall as the killer.

2   See "Washington Is Burning" by Andrew Cockburn in the September 2014 *Harper's*, although I strongly disagree with his criticism of Key.

3   See, for instance, *Triumphs of Experience: The Men of the Harvard Grant Study* by George E. Vaillant.

4   McCarthy, C. (2010) *The Cambridge Introduction to Edward Said*, Cambridge University Press, p. 19.

5   Winnicott and his 18 reasons for a mother to hate her baby (previously cited) comes to mind here also.

6   Some number required to reach the "tipping point" for social change.

CHAPTER 10

Monologue with Francis Scott Key

You ask us, Granddad, from your grave: "Does our flag still wave over the land of the free and the home of the brave?" And I respond: Yes, Granddad Frank, the flag is still flying and there are fifty stars on it now, which include Hawaii and Alaska. "The Star Spangled Banner," words and music, became our official National Anthem in 1931 and is played and often sung before many large public gatherings, such as baseball games and other sporting events. The same flag that you saw over the ramparts of Fort McHenry on that morning of September 14, 1814 — now 200 years old — has been preserved and restored, and is now a national treasure on view at a large museum in Washington. Many of us from different walks of life continue to share your concern for the status of freedom and bravery in our country. Because of years of research and study, we have a better understanding of human events now but your words still ring true, for even with the bravery and vigilance of concerned citizens, freedom is ever in danger.

We've made a lot of changes since your time: some planned, but many accidental, some good, some not so good. Remembering how you supported education for children, you will be pleased to know that, among the good changes, all of the children (boys and girls, black, white and others) get 12 years of free school paid for by the state. 85% complete the 12 years and 30% of these go on to earn college degrees. Another 11% attend and complete post-graduate schools. There are still private schools, some of which are religious in nature, but 90% attend the public schools. Of the 10% of students in private schools, 43% are Catholic and 2% are Episcopal.

Most voters today are middle class, which constitutes at least one-half of the population, depending on how it is defined. It is larger than the lower, working class or the upper class, although shrinking now due to economic changes. Women vote in elections and hold public office since 1920. Women vote in all countries of the world now except Saudi Arabia and The Vatican. Political fortunes still rise and fall from sex scandals as they did in your day with the Petticoat Affair.[1] Now at least we understand the main reason for the intense interest and outrage by the public in these sex scandals, and why publishing them in newspapers is good for the profits of editors. It is because they represent people breaking rules that the rest of us resent having to follow. We express anger toward the rule-breakers but part of our anger comes from having to follow the rules ourselves. Others are "getting away with" something.

Your brother-in-law, Roger Taney, lived to age 87 and served as Chief Justice of the Supreme Court for 28 years. He died in 1864 near the end of the Civil War (more later), on the same day that Maryland abolished slavery. While his record as Chief Justice is controversial (Dred Scott decision), you'll be pleased to know that in 1931, he was eulogized by another Chief Justice, Charles Hughes, in Frederick, Maryland, and a bust of Taney was unveiled there.

The economy still has its ups and downs, but all social classes are better off than they were 200 years ago, at least materially. Average life expectancy is now 78 because we have made vast improvements in medicine and public health. Very few infants die now. But even in your time (1850), if a child lived beyond age 10, he or she could expect to live to age 58.

Spiritual comparisons are more difficult to make but I believe we have regressed in that area. With more material resources available, the temptation increases to focus life on gaining more material wealth and neglecting spirituality. We seem desperate to have more than our neighbors because we fear losing out in some vital but mysterious struggle to survive and excel. When resources and entertainments are scarcer, as they were in your time, we seem to be more prone to cultivate our spiritual potential. Most people would be surprised to learn they were happier when they were poorer, but research shows that to be the case. We seem to feel we "know" the future better than the past and are easily convinced that some future material goal will finally bring us complete spiritual and material satisfaction. It seems we can be happiest when we anticipate a future event rather than when it actually arrives, always believing it will somehow solve all of our problems. Wealth is a disappointment and this is one reason we have replaced the idea of the "good life" with the idea of the "enviable life." Our new idea of the good life, perpetual happiness, is so unrealistic that it cannot be attained. We are not even satisfied to be better than our neighbors; we want them to envy us. This supports our hope that we are at least materially superior, and this is a hope that can sometimes be satisfied.

• • •

One of the best improvements since your day is that we now have year-round automatic heating and cooling systems for homes and buildings. Chamber pots and privies or outhouses have been replaced by indoor bathrooms and toilets that flush away shit with the turn of a handle. This is a further refinement on the practice of your day where the larger homes had separate stairways for servants so they would be less conspicuous and we wouldn't meet our chamber pots on the main stairways, (John P. Davidson, "You Rang," *Harper's*. Jan. 2014, p. 43 footnote).

We even have sinks and bathtubs with hot-and-cold-running water and, since rooms are heated, we can bathe in tubs or shower at an ideal temperature, even in the middle of winter. Each city has an extensive water supply system ensuring sufficient water for fire-fighting purposes, as well as abundant purified water for drinking and bathing for everyone. Water is piped into almost every home; we need only turn a handle (one for hot and another for cold) in the kitchen or bathroom for a steady supply of clean water at any temperature we desire. The average family in the U.S. uses about 70 gallons of water a day. Wastewater systems convey bathroom discharges to processing centers where the water is treated and purified before being released back into rivers and seas. Unfortunately, 14% of the world's population is still dependent on unprotected water sources, which are often sources of disease.

Streets are paved and lighted at night; mud, dead animals and chamber pot contents in the streets are a thing of the past. It is possible to walk for miles in a city and never set foot on grass or dirt. Because indoor air can be cooled, we can even cook indoors in the middle of summer without heating up the house too much. Cooking is done with stoves and ovens that can be adjusted to the desired temperature by simply turning a dial. Ice boxes that had to be resupplied by the ice man every day or two have been replaced by large containers that again, have dials for selecting a cold temperature — they even make ice! These kitchen devices make cooking, and the safe storage and preservation of food, easy and save many hours of housework. Canned foods are much more abundant than in your day and we've found ways to freeze and dry food as an additional way to preserve and store food safely for long periods of time. Many kitchens even have machines that wash dishes and clothes so that it is easy for dishes, clothes and people to stay "clean." We have found a way to convert the power of waterfalls and fire into electricity, which then can be transferred into cities over wires to operate all the machines and provide for streetlights at night.

The disadvantage of all of these "purified" activities is that it facilitates an attitude in people that they are superior to the dirty animals that stink and die, as well as other people who are not perfectly clean. There seems to be a belief that since we have diminished death, and made dirt and shit disappear, we have risen above our animal nature. We struggle to support the illusion that we have somehow evolved to a higher stage of being — more godly and spiritual, and of course superior to animals and other people not as clean as us. For a price of $7,000, we can even have surgery to remove the sweat glands from our armpits, so we no longer produce body odor there. It reminds me of the description of the Chagga tribe where the men wore a wooden plug in their ass to "prove" to the women that they didn't shit, and so were vastly superior to the women.[2] I imagine the women in the tribe pretending to believe the men to give them consolation, much the same way that some blacks in the South pretend to believe in white supremacy to give the white people consolation — which is love, or at least compassion.

I am retired now, but I used to work in something we call psychotherapy. I saw clients for an hour in my consulting room and helped them to talk about their problems and search for answers. There is another form of therapy called aromatherapy, in which people are exposed to different pleasant fragrances in order to improve their mental disposition. My own version of aromatherapy is to let the shit build up in the toilet and smell the "aroma" there. This puts us back in touch with our animal origins and animal destiny and helps us to appreciate more the wonderful interval in between.

Another disadvantage of all of these labor-saving devices is that very few people have live-in servants anymore, partly because of the expense; servants are paid more now so they too can have a better level of living. There are people who take care of children in the home, usually while both parents are away at their jobs, but these are seldom live-in servants and constitute more of a shadow-presence in the family. Cleaning people once or twice a week are common among the affluent but are even less significant in the family structure.

The drawback of this new social structure is that it greatly diminishes the contact across social classes. In the past, live-in servants often became more like another member of the family, thus providing an intimate connection between social classes. So now our understanding across classes is diminished. When my mother's family was in a quandary over how to pay for my divorced aunt's nursing school expenses in the 1930's, their live-in servant, Hulda, an immigrant from Sweden, volunteered to pay part of those expenses. It then fell to Hulda to raise my aunt's three children in my grandparents' home, while my aunt was in a dormitory at college. Hulda worked in the home for 45 years without a day of sickness until she was admitted to a hospital and died shortly thereafter. She did have episodes of anger when she told my grandmother she would have to leave. Granny would always say: "I will miss you, but do as you think best."

Hospitals are more numerous and better funded and staffed than in your day. Medical science has made tremendous strides forward. The pneumonia that killed you in 1843 would today be considered a minor problem for someone of your age; you would have been cured and out of the hospital in a couple of weeks. We are attempting to implement a low-cost healthcare plan for America, which will provide medical treatment for all social classes as other countries around the world, including Canada, have already done. However, the richer classes are fighting it "tooth and nail" out of fear it will increase their taxes.

Another convenience added since your day is that most tall buildings have elevators, i.e., box-like rooms large enough for five to ten people that travel vertically inside buildings; they transport people from one floor to another so they don't have to climb stairs. This architectural feature allows for the construction of very tall buildings, a few of which are over 100 floors high. The primary source of power for these elevators is, once again, electricity. Cities use lights to turn night into day and even many country roads and highways have streetlights, which make travel easier and safer.

The disadvantage of all these conveniences is that they separate us from nature and tend to create the false impression that we are in control of our destinies, that we are separate from other animals and the Earth and the unpredictable but natural flow of life and death. New York democrats in your time presented President Jackson with a carriage made from wood salvaged during restoration of the frigate, USS Constitution, or "Old Ironsides." This celebration of heritage and craftsmanship and horses provides a startling contrast to our new ultra clean, electrified, motorized and largely plastic society. You will be pleased to know that "Old Ironsides" is still afloat, now the oldest commissioned warship still afloat. It is tied up to a dock near Boston and is open to the public most days for guided tours.

• • •

Communication has been revolutionized. There are still newspapers as in your day, but since the 1920's we have had a device called a radio; it reproduces voices from far away so that a person can announce the news into a receiver in Boston, and it can be heard in places like San Francisco through the radio. They are so small now that you can carry one in your pocket and thus, always be in touch with the news, weather forecasts and even music. More recently, since the 1940's, we have added visual images so we can see the person telling the news as well. Almost every home has one or more of these machines now and whole families spend hours watching entertainment like plays and sporting events and even international news with scenes of wars. The average American spends almost 3 hours a day watching and listening to these devices. For many, it has replaced reading books because it is less challenging, easier and more entertaining. Companies pay to advertise their merchandise on these machines and that finances the operation, but tantalizes viewers into wanting their "magical" products. That is, the advertising implies that the products will bring a kind of satisfaction that does not exist.

We have a word we use when we want to refer to all of these different forms of communication that inform public opinion: the "media." The disadvantage of this prevalence of media in the family is that it creates a false impression of what everyone should expect from life. We watch celebrities flaunting magical commodities, seeming to be continuously happy and important — we have come to expect the same thing for ourselves. The children are even more impressionable and some of the advertisements are directed at them. We feel resentful and angry when we can't afford the products, or when we do acquire them but they fail to deliver the expected happiness. The programs must be designed to make people feel envious so they will then be inclined to buy the commodities advertised and/or displayed on the programs.

• • •

Another innovation in communication is called a telephone. When I was a boy, I used to play with two tin cans connected by a string in the bottom of each can; with the string stretched tight, you could hear another child as he or she spoke into one can while you held the other can to your ear. That toy has been around for a long time; you may even have played with one yourself. Inventors have come up with improvements on that basic design until now we can usually hear the other quite clearly, even without connecting wires and from the other side of the earth. Nearly everyone carries a pocket-sized phone and we see people walking with their children and talking to someone on their phone at the same time. It has become an obsession for many; they feel more important when engaged in an "important" conversation in the midst of other "unimportant" people.

The first telephone call from the East Coast to the West Coast took place in 1915, but that required connecting wires. The "wireless age" started in 1950 and is now worldwide. Only sixty-four years later, we can now call almost any person and any city in the U.S., simply by pushing numbers on our phones. One disadvantage of this innovation is that it tends to replace face-to-face intimate conversation. People are so wrapped up in their "performances," their numerous important "chatty" connections, that intimacy with others is neglected and threatens to become a lost skill. Since those nearby cannot see or hear the person we are talking to, they can sometimes be persuaded by our tone of voice that it is someone very important saying very important things. This seems to be part of our defense against anxiety; if you stay busy with superficial affairs, you won't be plagued by the larger questions of life and the difficulties of intimacy and despair, both of which may challenge our peace of mind. Another disadvantage is that governments have the capacity to listen to our conversations and even track the locations of our phones.

• • •

Families don't have as many children as you did 200 years ago, in part because very few babies die now (we understand disease better and have improved public health and sanitation) and also because we have a worldwide crisis of over population. Population in the U.S. — about five million in 1800 — rose to 106 million by 1920, and now, in 2014, stands at 315 million. Both China and India have even larger populations, and China has implemented a 'one child per family' limit to combat the problem. The average fertility rate in the U.S. is now about two children per woman. This should provide just a replacement quota of children. However, the population has increased so much due to rates higher than this in the past that even this number will result in an ever-higher total in the U.S. for some years into the future. The numbers should then level off, barring more increases from immigration. Total world population was about one billion in your time and now stands at eight billion, with growing concerns over the possibility of widespread famines and chaos in the future. There are 45 million refugees and internally displaced people in the world today.[3] There is also a worldwide warming trend and more erratic weather patterns making farming more problematic. And we have depleted much of the ocean's fisheries.

The standard (what we aspire to) and level (what we have) of living is indeed higher now, but most families (52%) have two workers or bread-winners to provide enough income to raise one or two children by those standards. Many women, even mothers of small children, are now in the work force, even though it is very expensive to secure child-care services for the children (unlike Canada where it is subsidized by the government). In your time there were extended families of various relatives living together so there was usually a family member available to care for children. Most families today consist of the mother and father and their children: what we call the "nuclear family." This facilitates, and is often caused by, moving from one city to another in search of jobs for one or both parents. It also creates a different ambiance for the growing children: less stability but, some say, more opportunity to develop unique personalities. In some families now (3.6%), it is the husband who stays home to care for children while the wife works. The deciding factor is usually who can find the kind of job the family needs to meet expenses. Many men still find it difficult to maintain their self-esteem in this new role: that "chilling thought" of not being important, of being forgotten, intrudes on consciousness. As the practice becomes more frequent it will probably become easier: "strength in numbers."

• • •

A dangerous trend in our distribution of resources is one that you are familiar with: the income of the top 10% has been increasing over the years much more rapidly than the middle or lower classes. This allows the rich to have a disproportionate influence on public opinion through the media and financing campaigns of elected officials. This is identical to the process you are familiar with in your time: the Bank of the United States making unsecured loans to editors and members of Congress to influence public opinion and legislation. We remember your admonition in your address at Fredericksburg on August 6, 1834, about the moneyed aristocracy: that we should beware of becoming "the purchased possession of a company of stock-jobbers and speculators" (quoted in *Francis Scott Key*, by Edward S. Delaplaine, p. 381). Thanks for the warning, Granddad.

With the help of large machines, all of the agricultural work required in America is now performed by less than three percent of the workforce. There is more food available in the world but because there are more people, there is still much hunger. In countries with abundant food supplies, obesity and its attendant medical problems are alarming issues. The United States has more obesity than any other country in the world. Because of the decreased need for farmers and farm labor, there has been a large migration of farmers and farm-workers into cities to find employment in factories and other urban settings. Only 18% of the population of the U.S. now lives in rural areas; many of these commute daily into cities where they are employed. Enduring and stable agricultural communities with extended families and religious convictions are a rare thing now; they have been replaced by the mobile nuclear family and city work. Typically there are frequent moves from one city to another in search of work or because of company transfers; this leads to weak ties to amorphous urban communities or none at all. My father worked for a large corporation. By the time I was eight years old, we had lived in four different communities, five different homes and I had been to three different schools. Higher divorce rates also contribute to family instability. Forty to fifty percent of marriages now end in divorce. I, myself, was married and divorced four times.

We no longer use horses for travel: instead, we sit inside a box-like machine with a motor that we start by simply turning a key. It is called an automobile or car and there are 250 million of them in the U.S. We direct the motion of these cars by turning a wheel on the inside. It's like a four-wheeled horse-drawn carriage except the driver can turn the front wheels from inside instead of the horses making the front wheels turn with the shafts of the carriage. Horses and horse-drawn barges, wagons and carriages have pretty much been replaced by these motorized vehicles of various types on the farms, highways, city streets and even the battlefields. There are four million miles of roadways in the U.S. now: 2.6 are paved and 1.4 are unpaved.

The disadvantage of this easy and swift means of transportation is that many people die or are injured in traffic accidents on the roadways. Not only are the drivers and passengers killed and injured, but half of the deaths are pedestrians, cyclists and motor-cyclists. In the year 2010, the death toll from traffic accidents in the U.S. was 32,885; worldwide it was 1,240,000. And this says nothing of the injuries and disabilities (physical and psychological) of the survivors.

We have passed laws to limit speeds to 60 or 70 miles an hour on many highways, and 20 or 25 on city streets; drivers and passengers are required to fasten "seat belts" which improve chances for survival in accidents. Most vehicles have "airbags" which inflate automatically from the impact of an accident and help limit the extent of casualties. But of course, neither of these safety devices improves the chances of the many people out-side the vehicles who are injured or killed. Speed limits do help, but people protest vigorously when deprived of the pleasure of driving fast (i.e., being important). People are required to pass a driving test and buy a license before they can drive but still, the death toll continues. Some people drive as though they were at war. It seems to be a technique for expressing frustration, power and anger. We even coined a special term for the extreme form: "road rage." My daughter was one of those death-statistics.

In recent years, we lose about 20 times more people from roadway accidents than we do from the death of our sol-diers in war. Accident rates for the young are highest. One fac-tor seems to be that the young unconsciously sense the fear of their parents and our society, add this to their own and try to treat that fear by demonstrating their bravery — driving fast or going to war are two ready choices that can feel, at least un-consciously, like treatments. Also, young people — lacking the guidance, acceptance and empowerment formerly granted by stable communities and their churches — drive recklessly in or-der to avoid "social death" or feel invisible and to "prove" that God or an imagined magical parent figure is taking care of them and hence, will not let them die. "Neglect breeds insecurity and fear of irrelevance," (Hedges, *Losing Moses*, p. 146).

• • •

Continuing with the disadvantages of progress, our vastly improved medical services include enormous quantities of drugs which much of our population use and abuse. Illegal drugs are also a problem but on a much smaller scale. In 2008, Americans spent 234 million dollars on prescription drugs and about 106,000 died from these drugs. About 10 to 20,000 die each year from illegal drugs. But this is just the "tip of the iceberg." This drug-use by so many reflects an inability of the population in general to accept and live successfully without escaping, at least temporarily, from the pressures of reality. Hence, this monolog with you is part of an essay I've entitled: "The Real Enemy is Reality." There have long been alcohol and tobacco to diminish the pressures of daily living, but we seem to need more and more relief as we become more affluent and less spiritual. Some people even continue to smoke excessively knowing as we do now that smoking causes lung cancer.

Drug companies exploit this weakness by selling drugs even when their own research shows negative results. In a recent court case, the new drug was responsible for about 55,000 deaths but the company only paid a fine; no one went to jail. This kind of exploitation of the people gets very little attention because the media is very much funded and influenced by drug companies in cooperation with other moneyed and powerful groups. This is, once again, a replay of your struggle with the Bank of the United States in Philadelphia and its minions. We remember also your brother-in-law, Roger Taney's warning lest we not become ensnared in "the worst of slavery, that of submission to the will of a cold, heartless, soulless, vindictive moneyed corporation," (Delaplaine, *Francis Scott Key*, p. 378). Your struggle was successful but the outcome of ours is still uncertain. Eternal vigilance is the price of liberty.

• • •

A transcontinental railroad was completed in 1869 and by 1916, there were 254,000 miles of railroad track in the U.S. However, corruption seems to be endemic to industrial progress: it has been estimated that shareholders paid about three times what the railroads actually cost. Trains still carry most of our cargo and many passengers, but have been overshadowed by private vehicles, trucks and flying machines. All of these machines are similar to the steamships and locomotives of your day except that the motors are more compact and powerful and they burn oil instead of wood or coal. Motors have become so small that you can even attach one to the back of a rowboat. There are exceptions to corruption: the Bronx-Whitestone Bridge in New York was finished in 1939 six months ahead of schedule and under budget, albeit administered by a public authority rather than "financial titans."[4] Trains have declined since their peak in popularity in 1916 due to lack of profitability; some railways are now owned by the Federal Government to preserve trains as a viable and cost-effective means of public transportation.

• • •

Vacations have become much more common today. Most wage earners with full time jobs get at least two weeks off every year so the family can "go to the shore" or mountains to practice leisure and recreation. He and/or she continue to get paid while on these vacations. Even the remaining churches no longer preach against leisure; it is often promoted as good for mental health just as you used to retire periodically to your family estate of "Terra Rubra," or "Pipe Creek" as you called it, to recover your strength and patience. Your house at Pipe Creek was damaged by a storm, but was rebuilt in the 1850's and is now listed on something we call the National Registry of Historic Places.

• • •

Knowing how much you liked horses — Rancho Washi-kemba — and horseback riding you'll be happy to know we have not abandoned those fleet footed and sometimes affectionate and beautiful animals. Horses are a rarity these days, compared to your time, but as of 2005 there were still about nine million in the U.S. This compares with 23 million in 1911 before the advent of so much motorized transportation and its tragic toll of deaths from accidents. I used to rent horses and ride in New York City's Central Park, but the last livery stable/riding school for that purpose closed in 2007. Now the worn-out bridal paths have been surrendered to the baby strollers, tourists, bicycles and runners. People would complain about the horseshit on the bridle paths and on the streets leading to and from the stable. It was as though, if we could hide all shit (like we have succeeded in doing with the human variety by our indoor plumbing) and become super-clean, we could then escape from our animal nature and all death, tragedy and confusion. There are still some horse-drawn carriages in Central Park in New York that can be hired for a ceremonial ride around the park but the city is threatening to ban those too — for similar reasons, I suppose.

We can still ride horses in Prospect Park in Brooklyn, but cantering is not permitted and you have to be accompanied by staff from the stable. Out in the countryside, however, there are still many private stables and livery stables and opportunities for riding there.

There is even an island in the Caribbean called Bonaire where I have gone swimming with horses. They have trained some horses, with the encouragement of the rider, to wade out into a bay and start swimming when they can no longer touch the bottom. Riding bareback in a swimsuit, I slide off to the side of the horse so as not to be too heavy and can feel the horse's muscles working in the water with my bare skin. The trainer, Bregje, however, has to swim alongside with a rope attached to the horse's head to help him turn in the water. Since the horse's front legs only go back and forth it can only swim straight ahead.

Left to his own devices he would go chugging off toward Africa!

You will be proud to know that my mother, Mary Eager Lloyd Cox, started a horse-show called the St. Martin's Horse Show in New Orleans in the 1940's as a benefit for St. Martin's Episcopal Church. We both had jumpers. Hers was named Leaping Lena so I named mine Little Liza. She was a good rider but, much to her chagrin, I was better than her in my first appearance against her in a jumping class. There are still many horse shows around the country where people come together with their horses to compete in various classes and both the riders and horses can socialize.

There are still 163 foxhunting clubs listed in this country and 11 in Canada though each club, like each horse, has its own personality. For some it has become largely a ceremonial pastime where the wealthy can proclaim their social status and make others envious. I used to belong to a very liberal club of mostly New Yorkers named Hidden Hollow Hounds. We hunted in New Jersey and we even broke the "color barrier" by having a black woman as a member. On a trip to Ireland, I rode with a foxhunting club that was more of a local community affair. The local parish priest rode with us, and some mothers and grandmothers were accompanied by children on their ponies. The hunt began and ended at a pub, and when I asked for water, was offered a beer.

There was a time in England when foxhunting was encouraged as a way for cavalry officers to stay combat-ready.

Hunting has now been banned in England, Scotland and Wales because of public protests over killing foxes with hounds, when foxes are no longer serious predators on farms.[5] They could have benefited from your negotiation skills. Cavalry troops and horses in warfare have been replaced by a variety of motorized vehicles and flying machines. Soldiers kill from greater and greater distances and seldom see their victims face- to-face anymore. We even have small remotely controlled flying machines that kill without our having to put "boots on the ground."

• • •

Recreational boating has increased in popularity; it's cheaper and less complicated than keeping horses and is frequently combined with fishing. The smaller boats can even be floated on to a trailer and taken out of the water by a vehicle pulling a trailer. Then we pull them home and park them beside the house when not in use. As of 1998, there were 75 million people participating in boating with 17 million boats in use. People owned 1.6 million sailboats. Canoes (my favorite) are numerous on lakes and rivers. The trend is for people to own powerful things that they have absolute control over. With motorized machines we can feel the control we lack in our own lives and attempt to own things that are bigger and faster than our neighbors' so they will envy us and we will feel superior. With horses, canoes and sailboats, we have to negotiate with uncertain temperaments and contend with the vagaries of weather. You will note that this is a trend away from nature and its' mysterious and unpredictable spiritual attributes and toward an artificial and human superiority and distance from nature.

Your granddaughter, Mary, (Elizabeth's fourth child who was only eight years old when you died) married Edward Lloyd VII in 1851. Thus, she married back into your wife's family two generations later. The great grandson (Edward Lloyd VII) of your father-in-law, Edward Lloyd IV, married your granddaughter. They lived at the old Wye House plantation on the Eastern Shore near Easton, Maryland, the Lloyd family home. They raised eight children, one of whom, John Eager Lloyd, was my maternal grandfather. The plantation fell on hard times with the abolition of slavery but was rescued and restored to pristine condition in the 1940's by a member of the family, Elizabeth Schiller and her husband, Morgan. The old family graveyard there, where Mary along with much of the family is buried, is still active and welcomes "home" family members.

As you were such an ardent Christian, you will be distressed to learn that the Bible and religion in general are not as important as they used to be; we haven't really found a spiritual replacement: something else that would help us to hold ourselves and the country together. While 78% of the U.S. still self-identify as Christians, only about 40% still attend church regularly. People still search for religious answers as illustrated by the 40% who have either switched religious affiliation or changed to 'no affiliation' or changed from 'no affiliation' to a religious affiliation, (Pew Research, *Religious Landscape Survey*). Most people seem to be captivated by the ideas presented on the media, which imply that with the right combination of power, commodities, physical beauty, cleanliness and self-confidence, we can be happy without any spiritual connections. I'm calling this the "celebrity disease" or "celebrityitis." This delusion, however, helps turn the wheels of our economy: people work long and hard with the expectation of attaining celebrity status.

Many churches stand empty or have been sold and converted into restaurants, stores and apartments. Men and women living together without being married is common now; only 49% of household couples are married. Religion has become a divisive factor as the remaining believers unite in support of one conservative cause or another: trying to exercise power in order to lessen the fear of social weakness or death, and to "turn back the clock." One unanticipated consequence of this waning influence may be that, with the diminished emphasis on Christianity, our concern and even compassion for people of other religions has increased. This seems to be supported inadvertently by the media that happily reports tragedies from around the world to keep us "entertained." This distracts us from more important news in our own backyard such as the corruption and various maneuvers at influencing opinion or "cognitive capture," here at home. But they do show us the human side of tragedies of people whose religion is unknown to us.

Your disagreement with Bishop Kemp over baptizing a sick infant highlights a conflict between the hunger for power and pleasure within the church hierarchy, and the spiritual needs of members of churches. Recent revelations of sexual abuse of children by Catholic priests have stunned religious people of the world of all denominations. The Episcopal Church is not immune to such travesties. For a short time, I was on the vestry of an Episcopal Church in Maryland. My wife and I were gratified when the priest there took an interest in our son, an adolescent with many problems. Sometimes, the priest would call at night and say Billy was with him and, if it was all right, he would sleep over. We began to suspect Billy had a drug abuse problem about that time, but never connected it with our priest. Years later, when Billy was on trial for the murder of another drug dealer, we found out the truth. Billy's mother had the records of his child psychiatrist subpoenaed for his trial and discovered that our priest was giving Billy drugs in exchange for sexual activities. This evidence probably rescued Billy from a death sentence. The priest subsequently went to Texas to teach at a boy's school. On August 10, 1973, he was found beside a lake where he had been water-tortured and then shot to death, presumably by Texas vigilantes.

• • •

The American Bible Society, of which you were a Vice

President for 26 years, is still fulfilling its main mission and doing well financially (net assets of $436 million in 2010); but it has changed its mission statement slightly and is supporting religious entertainment, like plays which can be watched on the media and in theaters, which dramatize and popularize stories from the bible. In 2013, they supplied about eight million bibles to the world; these included one-half million to Asia and 800,000 to Europe. Adding up all the different biblical information and assistance provided, as well as bibles, totals 127 million. The cost for all of this was 25 million dollars. They've been having some conflict and turmoil within the organization that is reflected in frequent turnovers in leadership. They need you back.

The American Colonization Society, which you helped to found in 1817, controlled the development of Liberia until 1847, when the legislature in Liberia declared the nation an independent state. The Society continued to publish the African Repository and Colonial Journal until 1919, and did not formally dissolve until 1964 when it transferred its papers to the Library of Congress. Today, Liberia is home to some 3.7 million people; English is the official language there, although over 30 indigenous languages are also spoken. The capitol is named Monrovia after U.S. President James Monroe who, as you know, supported the colonization. The colonists and their descendants, known as Americo-Liberians, led the political, social, cultural and economic sectors of the country, and ruled the nation for over 130 years as a dominant minority. In 1980, however, a military coup overthrew this leadership, which led to two successive civil wars with deaths between 250,000 and 520,000. Today the country is recovering from the wars, but about 85% of the population continues to live below the international poverty line.

• • •

There is a current of optimism in today's society that supports a desire for some kind of ultimate satisfaction isolated from the spiritual, from the tragic and mysterious qualities of life. When we go to church, or when we used to, the image of the suffering, dying Christ on the cross was a vivid reminder of the suffering and tragedy so prevalent in the world and in our own lives. Today, we attempt to run away from this; to deny it. Likewise, the image of the Virgin and child is a reminder of the mystery, pain and frustration of mothering, of our failure to be perfect parents. We seem to expect perfect control and perfection in all things. We all seem to know what a perfect mother would be like and the image of the Virgin, while it provides some solace as an object of perfection, also reminds us that our own mother and childhood lacked this perfection. This awakens painful feelings of anger and guilt.

We seem to prefer to abandon church and these spiritual quandaries, these painful reminders, and pursue chimeras of perfect material consolation. Commodities are so much easier to understand and manipulate. Most people in our society agree on their value and even imbue them with magical qualities; many qualify as fetishes. They are our new idols. Small wonder we lack spiritual content in our culture and in the successes that we do achieve. The overall lack of spiritual gratifications seems to leave us with a reservoir of anger.

Just how is it we participate in that mysterious development of a functioning (or non-functioning) person from that initial screaming mass of uncoordinated protoplasm? Sometimes we seem to get it right, but the mother/baby dyad and family is still mostly a mystery. One reason for the current decline in religiosity may be that going to church "flies in the face" of our delusions of perfection and happiness. It leads toward despair, which is uncomfortable, but in your day I think it was part of the way you faced the world and solved problems. Now, most people expect to be free of despair, anxiety and uncertainty by accumulating wealth and power — so they avoid Christianity with its reminders of uncertainty and tragedy. Some even resent the idea of a God that is more powerful than them; they seem to want to be God themselves. Our mental hospitals house many who fully believe they are Gods or Kings. Granddad Frank, does despair come partly from your belief that all things are God's will and yet there is so much suffering and tragedy in the world?

• • •

You may notice a trend in our new civilization away from nature. Machines have largely replaced animals and servants as a source of power and comfort; city-dwellers no longer raise plants or animals for food. We buy pre-packaged and canned food in stores without ever seeing the sources. Servants are rare and slaves (as a legal entity) are non-existent, at least in this country. People seldom die at home now, but instead go to some institution for dying which helps us to imagine lives without death. As I said, in the cities we travel miles without walking on dirt or grass; pavement abounds so we can stay super-clean. The scarcity of horses and leather-goods tends to separate us from nature as well. Even wood is not used nearly as much as it was in your time, but is still prized for framing houses and for furniture. We have a very abundant material called 'plastic,' which is an oil-based derivative and is used extensively in manufacturing and construction. This further fosters the feeling that we are no longer connected to and dependent on the natural world. Once again, the image of President Jackson in his horse-drawn carriage made of wood from the sailing ship, "Old Ironsides" (USS Constitution) makes a striking contrast with today's norms and values.

This seems to have created an atmosphere that encourages us to feel we can somehow escape from the tragedies and vagaries of life. We suffer from an unnatural attitude of non-human or superhuman superiority; but anxiety is always bubbling beneath this pretense, which results in some outrageous behavior. People spend enormous amounts of time and energy, for instance, on personal appearance — beauty treatments and stylish clothes. But any success is always short-lived; they must soon start over again with a new style of home-decorating or stylish car or clothes or new and enviable vacation place or pastime. The life-experience seems to be predicated not so much on what we have contributed to the world as on what other people think of us. If they are envious, we feel important and successful, as though death has somehow disappeared. Perhaps you, too, saw much of this kind of thing among the wealthy in your time. The main difference today may be just that with the substantial increase in resources and income, more people spend more time in this kind of behavior. But this preoccupation has resulted in the neglect of personal relationships and other concerns such as the realms of nature and spirit, beauty, love, and not surprisingly, death.

• • •

There has been a massive increase in pets since your time, mainly as a result of the increasing middle class and food resources. There are about 93 million cats and 77 million dogs in the U.S. This seems to be in part an attempt to counteract our usual isolation from nature and from other people. These are not work animals on a farm, but rather animals that eat canned food manufactured especially for that purpose and have no responsibilities other than to keep their owners company. The owners take the dogs for walks and frequently treat them as though they were people or children — sometimes as the perfect, adoring and compliant child they never had. Opportunities for personal connections with other people (formerly abundant in the extended family and community) have diminished as well as our skill in making friends, so the dogs and cats fill in as make-believe people. People watch a great deal of entertainment (almost three hours a day as mentioned) supplied by the media, which is safer than engaging with real people. We can always turn the machine off when it disagrees with us. Contacts with others may threaten our imagined sense of our own importance.

Freedom and equal opportunity is under attack by the rich by diminishing assistance to health and education programs and avoiding paying a fair share of taxes; not surprisingly, this is supported by the media, or at least, not sufficiently criticized. This is reflected in a kind of paralysis of government at this time. Much of the population is tranquilized with trivia, thanks to the media; but some say the media is just producing what people want and need. Many seem to be confused and even overwhelmed by the many conflicts between groups and values in our society and in the world. Their attitude seems to fluctuate from a sleepy lassitude (while being entertained and often drinking alcohol) to innervating anxiety, without an in-between stop at despair for serious contemplation.

Part of the problem is that there are so many different sources and interpretations of news (many private individuals publish their own versions) that it has become increasingly difficult to "mold public opinion" or to arrive at a consensus. A new invention called a computer (almost everyone has one) allows for storing enormous amounts of information in a machine, analyzing it in many different ways, and then making the results available to people all over the world for a very small cost. So we have an epidemic of publications that do make it more difficult to conceal what's going on anywhere in the world — but it is difficult to identify which ones can be trusted.

With all of these new conveniences, time savers and increased life span, I would like to be able to report an increase in our ability to solve social problems. Unfortunately, such is not the case. Negotiation, as in your day, is a secondary skill; anger and conflict still rule the roost. It even seems that people with more spare time seem to get more anxious and fearful. To counter this they search for more power and more diversions, choosing to humiliate others for a feeling of power and losing themselves in continuous mindless activities and trivia in order to avoid their fears.

ENDNOTES

1   The Petticoat Affair was a situation within the cabinet of

President Andrew Jackson. When Cabinet member John Henry Eaton married a woman whom the wives of the other cabinet members considered socially unacceptable, all but one cabinet member resigned. Andrew Jackson: "I [would] rather have vermin on my back than the tongue of one of these Washington women on my reputation."

2   *The Denial of Death* by Ernest Becker, p. 32.

3   September 2013 *Harper's* Index.

4   The phrase "financial titans" comes from a speech by FDR to the Commonwealth Club of San Francisco on September 23, 1932: quoted in *Plutocrats*, (p. 177) by Chrystia Freeland.

5   The humanitarian justification fades when we learn it is OK to poison the foxes.

CHAPTER 11

Monologue Continued: Warfare

I will try to bring you up to date, Granddad, on warfare. Since the War of 1812 (loss of life: between 7,000 and 24,000), in which you participated, we have been engaged in many other wars. I'm defining wars as conflicts in which at least 1,000 people, military and civilian, died. By that definition, the world has experienced at least 3,023 wars to date. There were probably more, but earlier records are inadequate or non-existent.

The controversy over the annexation of Texas was brewing before you died. Texas became the 28th state in 1845 with help from your old friend and client, Sam Houston, who was the President of the Republic of Texas. However, Mexico did not recognize the boundaries claimed by the Republic of Texas;

this led to war with Mexico in 1846, which we won at the cost of more than 19,000 men. In the subsequent treaty with Mexico, we added the land reaching from Texas all the way to the Pacific Ocean; this land eventually became six more states. Although we paid Mexico for this territory — with our troops still on their land — Mexico was hardly in a position to negotiate strenuously. Some people, including myself, are still embarrassed by this annexation of Mexican land, much as you would have been had we succeeded in taking some part of Canada during the War of 1812.

• • •

About 20 years later, the issue of Nullification (i.e. the right of states to nullify federal legislation they disagreed with), which partly got you involved in politics, finally resulted in a civil war (1861-1865). Scholars disagree on the cause: Northerners will usually argue it was the slavery question; Southerners say the real issue was state's rights, which started with the struggle over nullification in your day. My grammar school principle in Jefferson Parish, Louisiana, assured us the issue was state's rights. Also blamed was the allegation that Northern industry couldn't compete against the cheap slave labor of the South. Slavery has now been legally abolished worldwide but continues in illegal forms. Destitute families in Asia may sell a child in order to survive. The Northern States won the Civil War but at great cost of lives on both sides (about 600,000 total). All the slaves have been freed but have problems, as many people still consider them inferior because of their skin color, the stigma of slavery and some lower-class social attributes.

We understand better now the importance of childhood experiences for the formation of personality. Given the advantages of a middle- or upper-class childhood, black people (in spite of lingering racist attitudes) integrate into society and function as well as whites. Because our identity, the way in which we perceive ourselves, is so tied into what other people think of us, the lower classes of whatever skin color still struggle with feelings of low self-esteem. This often produces antisocial behavior — but the intent is simply to stand out in society, to be noticed and express their anger over what is basically a lack of equal opportunity, to be important and not to disappear socially, to avoid social death. This struggle can seem so painful to the person of lower-class origins that they abandon hope and succumb to criminal activity and/or drug/alcohol addiction. We're making progress with discrimination — we now have a black president.

One of the unanticipated consequences of the Civil War, in conjunction with scientific progress, was the decline in religious convictions (Drew Gilpin Faust, *This Republic of Suffering*, p. 173). The problem of theodicy was raised to a new position of prominence in terms of social awareness. How to explain the presence of so much suffering on earth if God is all-powerful, all knowing and beneficent has always been a religious conundrum. But in the Civil War, both sides worshipped the same God; most died in the belief that God was on their side, died largely because they thought God was on their side, and died in the hundreds of thousands. This made many question the validity of religion. Religion, in a very real sense, "enabled the slaughter," (Faust, p. 175).

We went to war again, 33 years later, in 1898. This time, war was with a weakened Spain. We acquired all her territories in the Western Hemisphere plus islands in the Pacific at a cost of about 11,000 dead. We helped Cubans gain their independence. The islands included the Philippines, where we inherited the native rebellion there; by 1913, when the last of the armed resistance ended, it had cost about 234,000 dead on both sides, civilian and military.

• • •

The next war we participated in is called World War I, from 1914 to 1918, although we did not enter that conflict until 1917. This was the first war to be fought using the world's new industrial technology to produce the best killing machines possible. It was basically a European war; Germany invaded France and in 1917, we sent troops to help the French and English to defeat the Germans. The cost was about nine million dead soldiers, 21 million wounded and ten million civilian deaths. Subsequently, an international organization called the League of Nations was formed to create a structure for negotiation, which could avoid such catastrophes in the future: a "Holy Family of Nations," to use your phrase. The U.S. Congress, however, refused to join the League, which was active from 1919 to 1946 and at one time had 58 member countries.

It saddens me to have to tell you, Granddad, that there was a pitiful dark side of warfare during this time. It was reported by Smedley Butler, a Major General in the U.S. Marine Corp who served for 33 years in conflicts all over the world. He described his role as a gangster for capitalism, leading military interventions into other countries so as to protect the interests of Wall Street, Bankers, American Oil interests, sugar and fruit companies and frequently undermining democratic governments in the process. He also detailed the enormous profits made by businesses during wartime. He is best known for a book he published in 1935, "War is a Racket." I had some personal experience with this collusion between the military and corporations when I worked for Westinghouse Electric Corporation for five years, ending in 1970. The Navy provided Westinghouse many lucrative contracts for equipment and the quid pro quo was that, in turn, Westinghouse hired retired Navy personnel. In a speech to an international meeting of engineers, I criticized the quality of the ex-Navy personnel we worked with. Well, that was the end of my corporate career at Westinghouse. At the time, I didn't realize I was "blowing a whistle;" I naively thought everyone just wanted to know the truth.

• • •

Tensions in Europe continued, partly due to a brutal treaty punishing Germany for starting World War I. The result was another world war beginning 20 years later in 1939: World War II. This time Germany allied with Italy and Japan, and our naval base in Hawaii was the subject of a surprise attack by the Japanese. That attack brought us into the war, which we fought on two fronts: the European and the Pacific. We concentrated on Europe first and, after Italy and Germany were defeated, focused our forces on Japan and the many islands they occupied in the Pacific. Japan surrendered in 1945. During WWII, there were about 100 million people in uniform representing 30 different countries. Total deaths were approximately 72,468,900.[1]

A more successful international organization, called United Nations, was modeled after the League of Nations and formed after WW II; it is still active and has permanent head-quarters in New York City. This organization has been instrumental in reducing the size of wars but smaller conflicts still caused many deaths: Korea — 1 million; Vietnam — 1 million; Iraq — .5 million, and most recently Afghanistan, where 2,000 Americans have died plus untold thousands of civilians. We have avoided additional world wars, but continue to get caught up in regional conflicts for uncertain reasons in which our men and women (yes, we now have women serving in the armed forces on battle fronts) are killed and wounded and severely damaged psychologically. I'm not listing the many wars around the world that we did not get involved in, such as civil wars in Liberia, Syria and other conflicts around the earth.

• • •

Again, historians disagree about why we continue to get caught up in various conflicts and spill the blood of our young people on foreign soil. Some say it is the defense of freedom around the world and to keep the enemy from our shores. Others say it is the pursuit of influence and power and to protect national and corporate interests and to influence global markets. This argument is supported by the testimony provided by Butler in "War Is a Racket." Today we identify this social structure as the "military-industrial complex" and we are better at recognizing its influence on legislation and policy in ways that will increase its opportunities for profits (for industry) and fame (for the military). As mentioned above, ex-military personnel may also be hired by corporations which increases their profits as well.

There are now so many powerful new weapons in the world that we could easily exterminate all life on earth in another war. "We are all nervously loquacious at the edge of an abyss."[2] I know that you felt the War of 1812 could have been avoided through negotiation and — judging from the reduction in our war-death-totals in the last 60 years and the persistence of the United Nations — we are finally getting that message. It still seems a great mystery to me just why we are, as a species, so prone to warfare — again, the 3,023 wars.

How do countries get young men to die in wars, in the thousands and even millions? I do not pretend to have an answer but only an interesting piece of the puzzle. It seems that infants have an uncanny way of sensing the problems of the mother; they tune in to the problems of father and siblings also, but at a later stage. The infant makes a "diagnosis" and even attempts a "cure." We see this most blatantly with the infant's smile.

Babies learn, probably by accident, but early on, that their smile pleases people; mother most importantly. It makes her feel better. Thus, the baby begins to improve his chances for survival by "treating" mommy's anxiety; he begins to ensure his future and "pay his way" in the world; he increases the odds for the continuation of his "life-support system" — by smiling.[3] My hypothesis is that young men diagnose the disease of fear in their societies and — motivated by the desire for their own survival — wish to show their bravery in order to "treat" their society's fear. They seem to sense that if this "social disease" of fear becomes severe enough, the society might die. This would be a simple holdover from infancy: find out what threatens your survival and try to fix it. I wish you were here, Granddad Frank, so we could talk about this.

Part of a parent's fear which children understand intuitively is the parent's fear of death. We have a saying: "If the parents have the courage to die, the children will have the courage to live." Unfortunately, Granddad, we are still a long way from achieving such a healthy family environment for our children.

"If the parent has the courage to die, the children will have the courage to live." To create the obverse of this: "If the parent does not have the courage to die, the children may feel some unconscious motivation to demonstrate bravery in order to treat the "disease" of their parents and society. Roxana Robinson, at a book-signing meeting for her new book, "Sparta," quoted one of the veterans of the Iraq War: "There comes a time in the life of every young man when he feels he needs to go to war." If we could be braver and diminish our fear of death, children would be less motivated to "treat" society by exercising their bravery in war. It would also lessen our tendency to violence in general, a la Ernest Becker. This is the adage that combats the war tendency. There is great bravery in society. However, the fear has a greater impact because it is for the most part unconscious; children pick it up and magnify it because they cannot identify all of its parts and dimensions. If we could admit to more of our fears, they would affect our children less.

In addition, there may be so much repressed anger in our population that we create opportunities for warfare to project our repressed feelings of anger onto others and then accuse them of hating us. "The empty vessel makes the most noise." This also works for conflict within societies.

Warfare is, in part, a reflection of the compulsion by many to make manifest some of the unacceptable anger they feel toward self and others. These socially taboo feelings get expressed in the character assassinations and other psychological violence that take place daily, but must be denied in order than we can remain acceptable to ourselves and others. A "good war," however, allows everyone to express hostility openly and even be considered patriotic. These are subtle and unconscious motivations, but may be just enough to push us over the edge to war when negotiation might have been successful. The "War Hawks" in your time were instrumental in precipitating the War of 1812. As you will recall, some of the New England states were so opposed to that war they threatened to succeed from the Union.

ENDNOTES

1 See www.secondworldwarhistory.com/world-war-2-statistics. asp.

2 From the last page of *Permanence and Change*, by Kenneth Burke, 1935.

3 Donald Winnicott describes a scene of a nursing mother where the baby raises his thumb to the mother's mouth. He attempts to return the "favor" of nursing and strengthen the bond. The power of the smile is illustrated in the opera, 'Turandot.' Prince Calàf's blind, old father is being cared for by his only remaining and faithful slave-girl, Liu. She explains her loyalty to Calàf's father by saying that when Calàf was a child he once smiled at her.

CHAPTER 12

Monologue Continued: Four Vignettes

I would like to share with you, Granddad, four vignettes from a two-year road trip I recently completed with my French-Canadian girlfriend, Diane Couture. I think stories about our land can add a different dimension to my report about our life and times today.

(1) First, in our travels we stayed for four weeks in a campground near Seattle, Washington where I became acquainted with Dan Hulberts, one of my friendly neighbors. Dan was a veteran of the Vietnam War, a war in Asia that we lost at a cost of some one million lives. In our frantic attempts to kill the enemy there, we sprayed tons of poison on the trees of the land to eliminate enemy hiding places. Only later did we discover,

in a painfully slow medical/political process, that these poisons not only killed trees, but civilians and our own troops as well. Because the killing of people was a long, slow process, and vested interests attempted to disprove the connection, it was years before the truth was established.

When I met him, Dan was dying from cancer as a result of his contact with that poison. He was still active and even invited me to go with him one night to watch naked women dance. Because of the treatment he was receiving for his cancer, he was impotent: this "watching" was the only sexual pleasure remaining for him. The following day I took him for a ride through a nature preserve to watch the "naked" wild animals roam virtually free on many acres of land, and with an easy and assured food supply. Dan enjoyed that show, too. Dan was brave. He told me that — even though he was dying of cancer from the war — he would do it all over again to keep the enemy from American shores. On two occasions, I went with Dan to the Veterans Hospital where he was being treated; the array of proud but disabled veterans I saw there was heart-rending.

• • •

(2) Diane and I also stayed at a campground in La Malbaie, Quebec, called 'Camping des Erables' (Camping in the Maples), with a wonderful view of the St. Lawrence River in the distance. We were there for three weeks and developed a friend-

ship with our very congenial host, one Jean-Jacques Tremblay. The campground is situated on land that he inherited from his grandparents who had farmed the land since the beginning of the 20th century. Small family farms are seldom profitable now and have been mostly replaced by agribusiness: larger and often corporate-owned farms organized on a business model for efficiency and profits. So Jean-Jacques left the farm and moved to the big city of Montreal, Canada, where he taught school for 32 years and raised two healthy children. He did not abandon his roots, however, but instead kept his grandparent's farmland and built this campground. Then, he and his wife, Louise, would come back when school closed for the summer months to operate the campground and reconnect with the land and some of his family traditions. He seemed to be constantly at work improving the campground including a number of intriguing pieces of outdoor sculpture. He truly enjoyed sharing the land with his visitors.

He is retired from teaching now and spends more time on the land. His brother sometimes occupies a vacation home nearby. It was heartening to experience this unique adjustment to our changing times. Most families from small farms have had to abandon the land altogether and move into urban environments bereft of connections with the land. Jean-Jacques informs me that soon he will have to close the campground and limit his activities. This is another pattern underlying migration to the cities; farms close because there is no one in the family willing and able to carry on the business. They will keep the land, however, and two rental houses so the two daughters will have a place to stay and continue the connection with the land.

• • •

(3) We pulled our trailer down to the Florida Keys and camped on Big Pine Key. Florida became a state in 1845. A very small type of deer live there, related to the White-tailed deer common on the East Coast, but about half that size, called Key Deer. It might have been named after you but instead, is named after the 'keys' or islands, strung out to the southwest of the tip of Florida. Since they have no natural predators other than the occasional wild dog — and it is unlawful to shoot them — many key deer are docile and hunt for food from people. They roamed freely in the campground where we stayed (the campground does not allow dogs) and one came up to me and sniffed me daintily to see if I had anything good to eat. We once saw a group of them wading in Mangrove swamps at twilight, foraging for food like some four-legged fairies drifting quietly in the fading sunlight and misty mixture of still water, plants, and sun-kissed air. They also eat flowers and plants from the yards of residents, a source of some consternation.

On another day while hiking in an undeveloped area of the Key, we came across about 15 corpses of Key Deer in varying stages of decomposition. Traffic-kills account for 30 to

40 deaths per year; this was where they were dumping the Key Deer killed on the one highway that bisects the island. There is a healthy population now of between three and eight hundred but their future survival is still uncertain.

• • •

(4) Finally, (you will see that some of what follows is conjecture, but the basic facts are true) we visited a museum, Centro Archeo Topo, in Les Bergones, Quebec. One of the displays there caught my attention. It included a photograph of the 7,500-year-old burial mound of a 12-year-old boy located on a lonely wind-swept and treeless mound in Labrador not far from the sea. This is the oldest known grave in North America. The nearby sea in this case was originally called 'Anse d'Mort,' or Bay of Death. Its name somehow changed over the years and became known as 'Anse Amour,' Bay of Love — a similar sound. But this conversion of death to love represents our constant unconscious effort to diminish the fear of death that haunts us all. [1] This fear is always present in societies but I believe it is stronger since your day. This is because we try so strenuously to hide it with so many schemes that it goes "underground" and expands because we don't talk about it. It just keeps coming back in disguised form, like going to war so we can put death away from us and onto the enemy. We have gained control over so many forces of nature that it encourages the hope that we can even

control death.

There were eight items of value found in the boy's grave: five weapons for hunting, two religious items and one personal adornment. These would have constituted all he might need in the "next life," but — judging from the preponderance of weapons — they anticipated a next life dominated by violence. These Maritime Archaic people came from the same small gene pool that we all came from: the 1,000 human pairs struggling to survive on the southern tip of Africa 70,000 years ago. They occupied Labrador for about 4,000 years. They struggled with much the same problems and tragedies as we do today. I imagine the young boy as a person of charm, beauty, artistic talent, bravery and a good negotiator; they occur now and then in all human communities. These "primitives" somehow lost this personification of the spiritual goodness of life, this symbol of love. Perhaps he even died on a hunt in the attempt to secure more food for his hungry tribe. The group was devastated.

They looked for a place of dignity and peace for their loved one's grave and chose this lonely, treeless and windswept mound as appropriate for his dignity and their grief. It was also a symbol of everyone's loneliness. Even the absence of trees recalled to my mind a famous French artist named Monet, who created a series of paintings with poplar trees bordering a winding river. For like those trees, we must all be stalwart individuals asserting our strength and independence. At the same time, however, we must proclaim our true existence as a part of a rhythmic process of unity with like-minded others over time and space. Each tree, like each person, is an individual and yet constitutes a continuum with past and future, space and each other. Perhaps the roots of the adjoining trees were even connected. Our bravery is necessary but not sufficient — we must have connections with other people in our lives. The tribe expressed their love and admiration by placing items of great value in his grave, which they also hoped would be useful to him in another life.

The cynic might argue that, no, they felt guilty for not having protected him better or for having transgressed against the Gods and decided to punish themselves by giving up precious items in order to alleviate guilt. I say no, there are some who are able to bring out the best in others; we should be more aware of that gift, cultivate it when discovered and encourage it in all of our young. Our tendency today is to reward those who are best at the manipulation and exploitation of others. Thanks Granddad Frank, for pointing us in the right direction.

• • •

Conclusion:

I hear your question, Granddad, from two hundred years ago: "… does that star spangled banner still wave over the land of the free and the home of the brave?" I have to tell you that bravery and love have been in short supply lately. They have been largely supplanted by a fear-based greed as many people search frantically for an uncertain kind of satisfaction — perhaps its' spiritual growth — but they seem to look in all the wrong places. They expect it, whatever it is, to come through wealth or fame or power (certainly not through despair, intimate connections with others, peace-making and contemplation); they expect it to provide some kind of continuous satisfaction and consolation and perhaps even glory. Again, we seem to "know" the future better than the past. Your spirit is still with us, Granddad, and many of us continue to search for the beautiful parts of the human spirit and for a truth and fairness that will benefit and strengthen the whole nation.

In our defense, Granddad, I must add that a different and more difficult form of bravery is required of us today. It has become apparent that life has no intrinsic meaning. Gone are your days when we could ascribe tragedies to a God's wrath and good fortune to his beneficence. We have had to accept that life comes with random tragedies, just as four of your sons died tragic deaths. Many people cannot accept this lack of an explanation for life; it drives them crazy. And this underlies much of the selfish and delusional behavior plaguing the world today. Many people cling tenaciously to the belief that some idol, a person, wealth, power, fame…. will relieve them of their anxiety and frustration. These frantic attempts at delusional satisfactions are killing our people and our planet. The accompanying anger produces an oppositional attitude to life when we should be cultivating respect and cooperation to harvest the best human experiences possible in the time remaining.

I wish I could have given you a more positive report, Granddad, but I know you want to hear the truth; thanks for caring and thanks for listening.

ENDNOTE

1   I think it's safe to say there were no real estate dealers around to glamorize the territory. Once, on the way back from a hot hike in the Hudson Highlands, I stopped for a cold bear in Cold Spring, NY. Asked by one of the bar regulars where I had been, I told him Mount Taurus. "Mount Taurus?" he responded; "Oh, you mean Bull Hill."

Bibliography

Becker, Ernest. *The Denial of Death*. 1973.

Bersani, Leo and Adam Phillips. *Intimacies*. 2008.

Bloland, Susan. *In the Shadow of Fame*. 2005.

Bradley, James.
   Flyboys. 2003.
   Imperial Cruise. 2009.

Chopra, Deepak. July/Aug. 2013 *The Atlantic Magazine*.

Conrad, Joseph. *Heart of Darkness*. 1899.

Davidson, John P. "You Rang," Jan. 2014 *Harper's Magazine*.
   p. 43 footnote.

Delaplaine, Edward S. *Francis Scott Key*. 1937.

Eigen, Michael. *The Electrified Tightrope*. 1993.

Faust, Drew Gilpin. *This Republic of Suffering*. 2008.

Frazer, James. *The Golden Bough*. 1890.

Freeland, Chrystia. *Plutocrats*. 2012.

Freud, Sigmund. *Civilization and Its Discontents*. 1929.

Goldstein, Kurt. *Human Nature in the Light of Psychopathology*. 1951.

Hansten, Phillip. *Premature Factulation*. 2009.

Harris, George. *Reason's Grief*. 2006.

Harper's Magazine. Index Sept. 2013.

Hedges, Chris.

War Is a Force that Gives Us Meaning. 2002.

Losing Moses on the Freeway. 2005.

American Fascists. 2006.

Keynes, John Maynard. *The Future, Essays in Persuasion*. 1931.

Key-Smith, F. S. *Francis Scott Key*. 1911.

McCarthy, Conor. *The Cambridge Introduction to Edward Said*. 2010.19.

Molotsky, Irvin. *The Flag, the Poet and the Song*. 2001.

Morley, Jefferson. *Snow-Storm in August*. 2012.

Orszag, Peter and John Bridgeland. "Can Government Play Moneyball?" July/Aug. 2013 *The Atlantic Magazine*.

Petrucelli, Jean. *Longing*. 2006; Chapter Four, Desiring by Myself, Adam Phillips.

Pew Research. *Religious Landscape Survey*. 2013.

Phillips, Adam.

On Flirtation. 1994.

Terrors and Experts. 1995.

The Beast in the Nursery. 1998.

Darwin's Worms. 2000.

Promises, Promises. 2001.

Going Sane. 2005.

On Balance. 2010.

Missing Out. 2012.

Robinson, Roxana. *Sparta.* 2013.

Steinbeck, John. *Travels with Charlie.* 1962.

Stossel, Scott; "Surviving Anxiety" Jan./Feb. 2014.

The Atlantic Magazine.

Styron, William. *Confessions of Nat Turner.* 1966.

Thoreau, Henry David; *Walden.* 1854.

Whitecraft, Mellissa. *Francis Scott Key.* 1994.

Winnicott, Donald. "Hate in the Countertransference" 1949.

International Journal of Psychoanalysis. 30. 69-74.

Also in *Collected Papers.* 1958. 194-203.

Yeats, William Butler. *Autobiography.*

About the Author

Early childhood experiences in cultural conflicts, and later, adult encounters with psychopathology in religion led Ted L. Cox to studies in sociology (including school desegregation in Georgia and Puerto Rican migrants in New York), and culminated in M.A. and Ph.D. degrees. During his research he encountered Ernest Becker's *Denial of Death*, which stimulated interest in unconscious motivation. This led to training and certification as a psychoanalyst.

At age 75, after ten years of experience as an analyst, he retired and began to write his memoirs, which benefited from a two year pop-up trailer road-trip with his partner. This book is the result of a lifetime of searching for plausible explanations for human behavior, explanations beyond the facile rhetoric of leaders, teachers and preachers with conscious and unconscious hidden agendas. This quest was aided and abetted by many encounters over the years with Mike Eigen's continuing psychoanalytic study group.

Cox lives alone in his Park Slope, Brooklyn, apartment and in Ste. Agathe des Monts, Quebec, Canada, with his partner, Diane Couture. They live in the Laurentian Mountains where they hike, film nesting herons, bike, canoe and skin-dive in the summer, and ski and snowshoe in the woods in the winter. For more details see: **blogdianeted.blogspot.com**.

Acknowledgements

Thanks to my long-time partner, Diane Couture, for unending help with computer science, and to Susan and Scott Brier of The WriteDesign Company for crucial editorial and design contributions. Diane was also the photographer for the author-photo on the cover.

I apologize to family and friends whom I have neglected of late in order to devote most of my energies to this book; especially my two sons, Ted and Kevin; my "daughter" Britt; niece Melissa; and friends Rick, Maria and Carolyn.